AN EVENING AT THE GARDEN OF ALLAH

★

BETWEEN MEN ~ BETWEEN WOMEN
Lesbian and Gay Studies
Lillian Faderman and Larry Gross, Editors

BETWEEN MEN ~ BETWEEN WOMEN
Lesbian and Gay Studies
Lillian Faderman and Larry Gross, Editors

AN EVENING AT THE GARDEN OF ALLAH

★

A GAY

CABARET

IN SEATTLE

BY DON PAULSON

WITH ROGER SIMPSON

NEW YORK ★ COLUMBIA UNIVERSITY PRESS

★

COLUMBIA UNIVERSITY PRESS

NEW YORK   CHICHESTER, WEST SUSSEX

COPYRIGHT © 1996 COLUMBIA UNIVERSITY PRESS

Library of Congress Cataloging-in-Publication Data

Paulson, Don.
    An evening at the Garden of allah : a gay cabaret in Seattle / by
Don Paulson with Roger Simpson.
      p. cm. — (Between men—between women)
    ISBN 0-231-09698-4 (cl)
    1. Female impersonators—Washington—Seattle—Interviews.
2. Impersonation. 3. Garden of Allah (Cabaret : Seattle, Wash.)
4. Gay bars—Washington—Seattle—History. 5. Music-halls (Variety-
theaters, cabarets, etc.)—Washington—Seattle—History.
I. Simpson, Roger, 1937–   . II. Title. III. Series.
PN2071.I47P38   1996
792.7'09797'772—dc20   95-42948

Casebound editions of Columbia University Press books
are printed on permanent and durable acid-free paper.

Printed in the United States of America

10 9 8 7 6 5 4 3 2 1

★

To all the gay and bisexual men, lesbians, and transgenders who kept the fires burning in earlier times, despite hatred and oppression, preparing the way for the victories of our time.

CONTENTS

★

PICTURES IN A STEAM BATH

★

I first heard about the Garden of Allah cabaret in Seattle in 1959. During the next thirty years, people told me so many times how fabulous it had been that eventually the Garden took on an almost mystical quality for me. I began to feel I had missed out on something very special. I had walked countless times on Seattle's notorious First Avenue in the 1940s and '50s, past block after block of peep shows, cheap taverns, and pawnshops, and past the Garden of Allah without knowing it was there. Like many young people I was trying to fit into society and looking for love at the same time. Someone could so easily have grabbed my arm and said, "I'm going to take you down to the Garden." It took me years to discover the diversity among gay and lesbian people; I could have learned about that in one evening at the Garden of Allah.

The Garden of Allah cabaret was the city's first gay-owned gay bar and one of the first in the country. It opened in 1946 in the basement of the Victorian-era Arlington Hotel, space that had housed a speakeasy during Prohibition and then a honky-tonk tavern. The Garden lasted a decade exactly; after the Korean War its exotic mixture of gays, lesbians, tourists, and servicemen gave way to edgy crowds of blacks and whites, young people fired up by blues and impatient with mellow ballads. The Garden's regular performers grew tired; it wasn't fun to create the shows anymore, and the audience noticed.

But in that decade the city's lesbians and gay men began to make a community. The first step was a group consciousness shaped both by prejudice and by the haven from hostility offered by the Garden of Allah. By the mid 1960s, a few were training for battle in the political arena, and by the mid '70s, city officials were taking notice and even listening to leaders in the gay and lesbian community. I believe that the Garden helped make that change possible. Safe from harassment because the cabaret's owners paid off the police, gays and lesbians schmoosed and cruised while the performers gave America's Tin Pan Alley culture a uniquely subversive flavor. Being "out" at the Garden in an oppressive time for gays and lesbians was a giant step toward having the confidence to form political groups, challenge police authority, and pound on the doors at City Hall.

In 1988, I heard that the late Jackie Starr, a popular performer at the Garden, had left some photographs to another Garden headliner, Skippy LaRue. I found LaRue where he works, at the oldest gay steam bath in America, the funky South End Steam Baths in Pioneer Square. LaRue, too busy to talk for the moment, handed me a big cardboard box. I sat near the swimming pool where naked men paddled listlessly and opened the box, which had been sitting in LaRue's garage for a year. The box held at least 250 photographs, most of them taken in the 1940s and 1950s. It was like opening a time capsule of Seattle drag history.

Nearly all the photos had some link to the Garden. Some showed servicemen in uniforms, boldly embracing the performers; in others, it was easy to spot the GIs and sailors in civvies. Servicemen's dress depended on whether the military had the Garden listed as off-limits at the time. Tourists and locals, most of whom were straight, grinned in delight at being snapped in such a naughty place.

But the most stunning photographs—large, glossy black-and-white prints— showed stunning women, beautifully dressed in elegant gowns or chic street clothes, smartly posed to convey their savvy, their confidence, and their knowledge that life is both bitter and sweet. For a moment I was captured by the fantasy, and it took me awhile to absorb the complex meaning of the pictures. I had known, of course, that the stars of the Garden were female impersonators. But as I lifted photo after photo and studied the magical way those men had transformed themselves into fantasy women, I was deeply affected. I was seeing more than just pictures of vintage drags; these were real people from a real place, but their lives were lost to us except for the old photos and, perhaps, the memories of the few who were still alive.

The spirit of the Garden had waited around for more than thirty years to snag someone to tell its story, and suddenly I knew that I was the one. I decided there by the swimming pool to answer the question: "What was the Garden of Allah?"

Skippy LaRue, who had been the catalyst among the Garden performers, became my main informant. We've spent untold hours going over the stories of everyone from the organists to the stars. I set out to interview other performers and anyone who had frequented the Garden. It was not always easy. I'd get a phone number only to learn the person had just died, or I'd spend months trying to track someone down. I've traveled to California and Minnesota for interviews. But ultimately more than forty people talked to me at length; more than one hundred people contributed stories, ephemera, and bits of information.

The interviews were marvelous excursions into the ways Seattle's gay men and lesbians experienced the 1940s and 1950s. Most people clearly enjoyed sharing their stories. A couple of people refused to talk about that part of their lives, and a few asked not to be identified; they are introduced in the book by stage names or by pseudonyms. Because the Garden is a metaphor for the unfolding of Seattle's gay and lesbian political community in the 1950s, I've included some details about how gays and lesbians lived and loved in the decades before and during the Garden's history.

My interviews yielded nearly one hundred hours of tape. I have edited the transcripts drastically to focus on the Garden, the performers, and the audience. The speakers' words are written as they spoke them, but details of the interviews, in some cases, have been rearranged to provide a narrative flow. The tapes, photographs, and related material will be given to the University of Washington Library's Manuscripts Division after publication of this book.

N.B. Two comments about the terms I use: first, I have used the term "female impersonators" throughout the book to refer to the men who performed in the Garden of Allah. They called themselves female impersonators; the words "drag" and "drag queen" came into use after the Garden's day when performers' voices were silenced and replaced by recordings. Second, with one exception I have used the masculine pronoun to refer to the performers. Many female impersonators and people who dress in full drag prefer being referred to as "she" whenever they are portraying women. Out of drag, they are comfortable with "he." The exception is Hotcha Hinton, who lived in drag, on and off the stage, and was always "she" during my interviews with people who knew "her." In fact, Hotcha was infuriated by the male pronoun and such terms as "mister." Accordingly, Hotcha Hinton is "she" in my book. In the interviews, I've respected the pronoun choice of the person who gave me information.

Here, then, is the story of the Garden of Allah, told by its stars, cast, and fans, and illustrated with a treasury of photographs from Jackie Starr and others. The Garden is the string and the interviews and photographs are the beads. The Garden's female impersonators strutted a tiny stage, offering an ages-old illusion. They were and are fascinating people, mostly ignored in our social history. Their stories explain how a cabaret acquainted and united the city's gays and lesbians.

ACKNOWLEDGMENTS

★

I want to express my special thanks to the late Mark Dempsey, actor and theater historian. His insights and technical suggestions will last me a lifetime. He also compiled the mosaic of Hotcha Hinton's life in chapter 8.

In addition to those persons who are named in the text, I want to acknowledge the assistance of Fred Ball, the Bengston family, Elizabeth Barlow, Stephen Blair, De Lois Bostick, David Buerge, Jeffrey Cantrell, Olive Carl, Bob Carter, David Coleman, Ray Cramer, Chet Donnelly, Dee Dorneck, Paul Dorpat, Richard Engeman, Mary Fager, Leslie Feinberg, Tom Flint, Marsha Foster, Harvey Goodwin, Anne Gould, John and Lael Hanawalt, Hal Hanson, Ted Herried, Anthony Howliet, Jim Kepner, Robert LaVigne, Bob McFerron, Bill Meclane, Joan and Vern Meryhew, George Muzzy, Paula Nielsen, Corky Parmenter, Ann Petit, Margaret Randell, Kay Reinartz, Leon Remillard, Diane Scott, Art Simon, John Stamp, Kitty Star, Marvel Stewart, Mona Thomas, Paula Trent, Avery Willard, and the Special Collections Division of the University of Washington Libraries, Eugene Neville, who provided additional photographs, and the Old Seattle Paperworks.

Juanita Paulson, my mother, and Rosa Youngblood, my grandmother, provided valuable support and love in my early years.

Lillian Faderman encouraged me to propose the story to Columbia University Press and Ann Miller, my editor, kept me going by showing that others also saw the value of preserving the story of the Garden of Allah, and made important suggestions about the text. Patricia Dinning provided invaluable help with the preparation of the manuscript.

AN EVENING AT THE GARDEN OF ALLAH
★

OPENING NIGHT AT
THE GARDEN OF ALLAH

★

Fred Coleman and Frank Reid, two gay men, opened the Garden of Allah cabaret in downtown Seattle in early December 1946. (Coleman quickly landed in prison for earlier tax evasion, and was replaced as owner by another gay man, Frank Carlburg. Reid was then about thirty-five; Carlburg was in his fifties.) Coleman, a visionary gay entrepreneur, and Reid had dreamed of creating a Seattle cabaret featuring female impersonation and they chose a venerable site for their enterprise, a grand Victorian-era hotel that had grown somewhat seedy and tarnished but contained a basement space well known in the city. The Garden of Allah had been a popular drinking establishment for the previous twenty years, first as a speakeasy, then after Prohibition as a tavern.★ Many of the Garden cabaret's first-night patrons on that cold December evening must have felt at home as they approached the classical Greek marble archway at the south end of the old Arlington Hotel on First Avenue.★

It had snowed the day before and the light dusting still lay on the streets. The hotel's lobby entrance also gave access to the white marble stairway that led down to the Garden of Allah. At the bottom of the staircase, patrons each passed $1 through a peephole, then opened a wooden door to enter the club. That night the Garden's first patrons saw the wonderful traveling female-impersonator gala from Miami, "The Jewel Box Revue." The opening brought together the Jewel Box's founders, who had set out to restore the faded art of female impersonation, and the Garden's gay owners, who knew the impact of female impersonation in San Francisco and other cities and had decided from the start to make the art the Garden's trademark. Soon the Garden would employ a regular cast of imperson-

★Fred Coleman was one of several investors who had interests in the Spinning Wheel, a tavern with a mixed straight and gay crowd, in the late 1930s and 1940s.

★The hotel was torn down in the early 1970s, and its site remained undeveloped at the end of 1994. The new Seattle Art Museum is across the street and in the next block north.

★ The Arlington Hotel opened in 1894, the first major building constructed as developers expanded northward from the zone destroyed in the great Seattle fire of 1889. The Cafe Arlington sign, at left, is over the entrance to the hotel and, later, to the Garden of Allah. (Photo by Asahel Curtis, Special Collections Division, University of Washington Libraries)

ators who would produce their own shows and backup appearances by impersonators from the national circuit.

The city's first cabaret owned solely by gay men quickly attracted a loyal and enthusiastic gay and lesbian following. The owners wanted to attract tourists, just as Finocchio's in San Francisco did, but unlike that cabaret, gays and lesbians always were assured respect and priority at the Garden. In 1946, the Garden's tiny 1890s ceramic floor tiles and dark-stained wainscoting were trifling anachronisms, details that briefly annoyed the postwar moderns who quickly forgot them as they gave in to the mad swirl of the evening. For most of those young people, World War II had given them opportunities, either in the services or in the cities that housed the defense industries, to explore sexual openness and same-sex companionship. Few really thought about or knew much about all that had taken place in the previous half century to create a Garden of Allah where lesbians and gays could meet safely.

THE GARDEN SPEAKEASY: AN EARLY SANCTUARY

A great fire had leveled Seattle in 1889, so the city at the turn of the century was a new one, reflecting the profits of outfitting the Klondike Gold Rush and the Spanish-American War. Seattle was a little New York City, rich with texture and variety. Wonderful Victorian buildings dressed up the avenues. Streetcars rumbled up and down the streets. During the day Seattle was full of commercial hustle and bustle and at night the clubs, theaters, dance halls, and restaurants throbbed with excitement.

First Avenue played the role it had played since the first settlers arrived half a century earlier. The avenue and the Pioneer Square district to the south attracted men, whether they were straight or gay, to drink, gamble, and find sex. Pioneer Square remained the lowest part of town—in elevation (it was right at water level) and in morals. Its name changed regularly, reflecting its notoriety and civic anxiety about its popularity: Skid Road, Down on the Sawdust, The Lava Beds, White Chapel, Black Chapel, Below the Deadline, The Tenderloin, The Great Restricted District, and so forth. Seattle was the sin capital of the Northwest, and First Avenue, especially around Pioneer Square, was the street of relief for hordes of single men.

The Arlington Hotel sat beside that sinful First Avenue, midway between Pioneer Square and the uptown, upper-class commercial center marked by its department stores—Frederick & Nelson and the Bon Marche. The hotel, designed by the noted architect Elmer Fisher, opened in 1894. Rated "first class" at the time, the hotel proudly advertised "Electric Lights, Baths, Elevators and Steam Heat." At first, the Arlington Cafe served the hotel's guests in the south end of its basement level, the space the Garden of Allah cabaret would occupy. By 1916, the Arlington Cafe had given way to a Brunswick billiards hall.

In 1926, Mike Schaffer opened a speakeasy on the site and gave it the exotic name, The Garden of Allah. The name was an easy choice at the time; that was the title of a popular 1904 novel by Robert Hichens that was adapted for the stage in 1911 and made into a movie a year before the speakeasy opened.[*] Moreover, in his celebrated role in *The Sheik* (1921), the androgynously appealing Rudolph Valentino brought the popularity of Middle Eastern exoticism to extraordinary heights, and Arab fantasy became a staple of American popular culture.[*]

By 1926, speakeasies had sprung up in cities large and small, in defiance of the constitutional amendment ratified in 1919 prohibiting the manufacture or sale of

[*]The story was filmed again, with sound, in 1936, starring Marlene Dietrich.

[*]A year after Schaffer opened the Garden of Allah, the lesbian actress and silent screen star, Alla Nazimova, created the infamous Garden of Allah hotel in Hollywood. The hotel was to become a haven for a talented and eccentric cast of guests and movie stars—many of them homosexual—of Hollywood's golden years. There also was a 1915 song, "The Garden of Allah," featured by a famous impersonator, Francis Renault, among others.

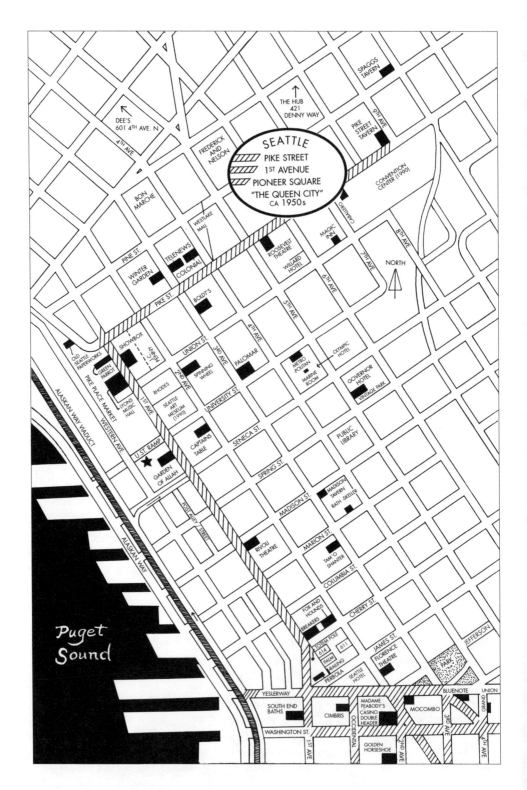

★ In the Garden cabaret's day, downtown Seattle was anchored by Pioneer Square, the rowdy site of the city's birth, and uptown attractions such as the Pike Place Market, the department stores, and the Arlington Hotel. The map shows the businesses that attracted gays and lesbians around 1950. (From map by Don Paulson)

★ William Hoey, a straight actor who played Dame roles in vaudeville, was photographed in 1889. (Photo courtesy Mark Dempsey)

intoxicating liquor. Those ubiquitous outlaw enterprises frequently served as sanctuaries for gay men and lesbians, and especially for the ultimate social outlaws, female impersonators.

Female impersonators appeared in speakeasy floor shows in Seattle in the 1920s, but they had been preparing the way since the Victorian era. Ted French and Frankie Kumagi, life-partners for nearly fifty years, told of hearing a Seattle impersonator reminisce in 1950. They recalled his words: "Darling, drag is not new. I was doing drag and singing and dancing in clubs up and down the West Coast since 1890. Oh, we had our

★ Fred Atwood toured Alaska and the Yukon Territory in 1903 in a classic comic opera, *Erminie*.

bustles and pinched ourselves into those horrible corsets, and picked up sailors coming in off the ships."

Speakeasies in other cities were often run by gangsters. (Jackie Starr, later a headliner at the Garden of Allah, told friends he and James Cagney had danced in the chorus line in a mob club in Chicago—both in drag. One night a mobster in the club discovered Starr wasn't a woman, drew his pistol, and started shooting up the place. Starr and Cagney escaped in the confusion.) The mob never got much of a foothold in Seattle because the police already ran a tight protection system, for which they expected regular payoffs from speakeasy operators. They were not about to let anyone muscle in on their turf.

The speakeasies and their second cousins, the burlesque houses, all operating under the police payoff system, protected young gay men as they "came out" in the limited

★ Julian Eltinge's Vaudeville Review played the Metropolitan Theatre in Seattle in June 1919. (Special Collections Division, University of Washington Libraries)

gay world of the time and as a few bravely crossed gender lines to live, at least part of the time, in a female identity. In the 1920s and '30s, a homosexual underground flourished in Seattle. By the late '30s, Jimmy Kelly knew a circle of about forty gay and lesbian friends, in addition to forty or so gay people whose lives revolved around Pioneer Square.

Vilma, a gay man who began to cruise Pioneer Square in 1930, recalled that young gay men went to Seattle burlesque houses in the 1930s to cruise and to watch the women dancing in the line. The queens—the gay men—and the women in burlesque were always friendly and would go together to speakeasies after the shows. Sometimes, men would be hired to join the chorus lines in drag to dance and even to strip, although the secret was usually kept from the audiences. (In one show in the Palm Burlesque Theatre in the early 1930s, the men watching one stripper erupted in laughs and screams, leading a cop who was standing in the back of the theater to rush up to the stage to see what was going on. Vilma recalled that the dancer finally looked down "and saw one testicle exposed from her shorts. She didn't blink an eye and carefully and delicately tucked the testicle back in her shorts and went on with the show.")

The earliest known gay hangout in the city was the Casino, a straight cafe, pool hall, and cardroom opened by Joseph S. Bellotti in 1930 and operated by John and Margaret Delevitti. The Casino opened in the same space as the notorious Klondike Gold Rush boxhouse, John Considine's People's Theatre. (A boxhouse was a theater attached to a saloon; the theater boxes were used for prostitution.) Gays also frequented taverns, restaurants, pool halls, and steambaths that would tolerate them. Some were part of the gay and straight intellectual crowd that surrounded the Pacific Northwest School artists Morris Graves, Mark Tobey, Bill Cumming, and Guy Anderson at such respectable places as the Rathskeller Tavern. Boldt's Cafeteria next to Woolworth's Department Store on Third Avenue was a regular spot, as was the Spinning Wheel cabaret. But all these places were straight-owned and run primarily for straight customers.

Max Newberry recalled what the Garden of Allah speakeasy was like about 1930: "A friendly couple owned it; she was the matron at the door. They issued us a card with our real names on it. A small band played for dancing customers and a floor show. They had plenty of sailors and always a lot of gay people. You didn't tell many people you went there, especially in the 1930s when they began to have female impersonators in the floor show."

Female impersonators performed at the Garden and some in the audience might be in drag. More attractive than most speakeasies in Seattle, the Garden was a favorite of both straight and gay patrons and prospered until Prohibition ended in 1933. Jack Cordas, who owns Seattle's oldest business, a western clothing store, went there because he loved to dance. "Once I danced with a female impersonator at the club, but I didn't know it. It was a 5/4 time dance. When a man can follow 5/4 time that's pretty good."

Norman Knudsen, who sometimes played the organ at the Garden speakeasy for a meal, recalled the hotel's midtown location was well suited to the secretive encounters encouraged at the Garden. "The patrons didn't cause attention when they left the Garden; they paired up or did whatever they did in private and that's all there was to it. The newspapers left it alone; they didn't bother anybody so it didn't cause controversy. The boys would be dancing around with their hands in another one's pants and patting each other on the butt. When I went down to the Garden I did not get into conversations and I kept my hands in my pockets. It was way out of my lifestyle."

Indeed, the big pipe organ lured many musicians to the speakeasy and many of the best organists in the region placed their hands on its keys and a foot on the volume pedal. The organ at the Garden was an orchestral Wurlitzer, seven sets of pipes, response as fast as a piano, and sound large enough to fill a theater auditorium. The mechanism was the finest you could get at that time and the response much faster than other models. Built in 1924, according to Wally Stevenson, and probably salvaged from a movie theater after soundtracks made the auditorium organs obsolete, the Wurlitzer served the Garden until rats craving the animal glue in its pneumatics damaged it in the last days of the cabaret.

The Great Depression increased racial and sexual discrimination and political and social unrest. Conservative forces, led by the Catholic Church, took charge of movie content, making sure that gay men were seen, if at all, as sissies.* Female impersonators felt the same backlash that stopped Jewish comedians from using their kind of ethnic humor. A vicious echo of the hate campaigns of Nazi Germany, white Americans, spurred on by some newspaper publishers, radio preachers, and politicians, attacked Latinos, blacks, and Asians, as well as gays and lesbians, who had become more visible in the 1920s and '30s through fiction and drama. In many parts of America, female impersonators were barred from the popular stage.

After Prohibition ended at the close of 1933, the Garden of Allah became a honky-tonk tavern. Speakeasies had flourished because of their illegal status; police protection provided stability that the competitive marketplace often does not. The legal taverns that succeeded the speakeasies found less money and a horde of new competitors. Moreover, the change added a layer of bureaucratic city and state regulation to the continuing squeezing of tavern owners for payoffs by the police vice squad. The fancy shows, including the female-impersonator routines, disappeared, replaced in the noisy and garish honky-tonk taverns by jukeboxes and "B girls," women who earned a small cut every time they persuaded a customer to buy a drink and sometimes used the bar to contact men for prostitution. Taverns offered cheap drinks, though, and some in Seattle were friendly to everyone, including gay men in drag. Such guardian angels usually had to deal with the police in order to keep the doors open to gays and lesbians. Owners profited from accepting diverse people, of course, but often they had to be courageous and tough to welcome some many in the community had rejected.

Orv Buerge recalled being a sailor on the town in 1934. "We'd been on that ship a long time and we were anxious to have ourselves a little fun. We got off the ship and walked up the University Street ramp and up the street to the Spinning Wheel. They had a floor show going on and we watched this good looking gal, Billy Richards, sing her song. Then we found out she was a female impersonator. She was made up in gowns and jewelry and all that crap. We just looked at each other and walked out. We said, 'To hell with those queers,' and went down the street to the Garden of Allah and I'll be damned we saw some female impersonators down there! It was a straight tavern but they let them come in there."

With the coming of war, the Garden's fortunes rose along with most businesses in the seaport city, long known as a shipbuilder, that was also soon to be a major maker

---

*Vito Russo, *The Celluloid Closet* (New York: Harper & Row, 1981), especially pp. 3–59; Garth Jowett, *Film: The Democratic Art* (Boston: Little, Brown, 1976).

of aircraft. The tavern became known as a "sailor bar," because it attracted servicemen stationed at the new or activated military bases in or near Seattle or waiting to be shipped out, and gay men, who might hope to pick up servicemen.

A GAY COMMUNITY TAKES SHAPE

World War II set the stage for the emergence of strong gay and lesbian communities in America's urban centers, especially in coastal cities such as Seattle. As Allan Bérubé has shown, the mobilization for the war freed gay men and women from "silence, isolation, and self-contempt."* Hundreds of thousands of gay men were drafted into the services or volunteered for duty; an unusually large share of the 150,000 women who served in the military were lesbians. Many of those identified as lesbians or gay males were given noncombat assignments; those hounded out of the service for their homosexuality often discovered new support among other gays. Gender segregation during training easily allowed gay men and women to find and acknowledge others like themselves, and port cities like Seattle offered havens for social contact off base and opportunities for romantic hours or days together during leaves or before shipping out.

Seattle became an industrial city in the process of helping to build an air force and navy adequate to the need. The city's labor mobilization drew workers from all around the country, liberating additional thousands of lesbians and gay men from the isolation of smaller towns and cities. A large share of the new wage-earners were women, many of whom were single and had moved away from small towns. In wartime Seattle, lesbians found work making bombers and protected social contact in airplane assembly plants, segregated hotels, and private homes. At the end of the war, many homosexual defense workers chose to stay in Seattle, joining lesbians and gay men who had seen Seattle in their service time and decided to move there after discharge.

As their numbers grew, Seattle's gay men and lesbians devised ways to meet that were relatively safe. Such protected meetings not only permitted romantic alliances, but allowed men and women to begin to explore the condition of being gay or lesbian consciously. Bars, after-hours clubs, and parties allowed men and women to meet freely. For many gay men, though, cruising had developed into an art form in an era when there were few sanctioned ways of meeting other men for sex or companionship. Cruising took place on streetcorners, in bathhouses, public restrooms, city parks, and all-night movie-theater balconies (which separated men and women). In Seattle, choice pickup spots were the Winter Garden, Colonial, and Green Parrot (also known as the Dirty Bird) movie theaters, and parks where tunnels through dense bushes facilitated encounters. Servicemen could be picked up at any bar, gay or straight, as long as one remained discreet. Cars steadily circled the block once occupied by a J. C. Penney department store. And the Greyhound bus station, like all the others around the country, was a risky, but popular spot.

*Allan Bérubé, *Coming Out Under Fire; The History of Gay Men and Women in World War Two* (New York: Free Press, 1990), p. 256.

Working-class lesbians formed their relationships in different ways. They were more likely to meet in their jobs or in social settings, such as church or neighborhood gatherings, although a few women also met in bars. Athletic women joined city-sponsored "fast-pitch" softball teams or played in basketball leagues. A few joined motorcycle clubs. Denied some of the freedom of movement men enjoyed, women found it harder to form relationships, and couples stayed together for longer periods. The social institution that best supported the lesbians was the house party. Seattle women said they went to house parties as frequently as once a week, and emphasized that the parties were attended mostly by lesbian couples in long relationships.

Lesbians were highly conscious of their roles. "These were the days of butch and femme," according to Pat Freeman, who is a program manager in Boeing's maintenance training department. The butch's role was to make love to the femme and "be the man of the house," she said. The femme had to be passive. In groups as well as in bed, the role-conscious lesbians seemed to be trying to live up to the expectations fostered in the straight community. Butch and femme roles were tightly defined, and anyone who defied the role was a subject of gossip and derision. "Unfortunately, the sexism of the period was emulated, too," Freeman said.

In the 1940s, young lesbians began to break out of rigid role-playing. The older women would be shocked, Freeman said, when a butch would leave a femme to be a femme to another butch. Some of the young lesbians rebelled against the isolation they experienced as teenagers when they were often frozen out of social networks because older women ran the risk of jail for associating with underage women. Committed women were so numerous that single women often had to find new partners by attracting those already in relationships. Indeed, some women gained reputations for breaking up established couples.*

Gay male roles also were influenced often by straight stereotypes. "Queen" was the term for a gay man who was the passive partner—or "bottom"—of a very masculine gay or straight man, or "butch." The role-playing dictated that a butch and a queen pair up, parroting the man-woman pair in heterosexual relationships. The roles weren't always maintained, however; ki-kis were queens who had sex with each other. Other queens ridiculed ki-kis, and said they were "piss elegant" or part of the "cuff-link crowd" because they gathered in elite, safe straight havens such as the Marine Room in the Olympic Hotel. The issue sometimes brought into conflict the rigid working-class role-playing and the more casual assumptions of upper-class men. The common put-down from a role-playing queen to a ki-ki was, "What's the matter, honey? You can't get a man? You have to go out with your sister?" The recollections I heard about such exchanges had that judgmental tone even though both working-class and upper-

---

*Freeman's emphasis on the imitative character of lesbian relationships is echoed in some recent studies, but not all. Faderman acknowledged that some lesbian historians found the roles to be unique and evolving, but she also noted the direct reflection of working-class male and female styles. Lillian Faderman, *Odd Girls and Twilight Lovers* (New York: Columbia University Press, 1991), pp. 167–74. The agency of such roles is elevated in a more recent study: Elizabeth Lapovsky Kennedy and Madeline D. Davis, *Boots of Leather, Slippers of Gold: The History of a Lesbian Community* (New York: Routledge, 1993).

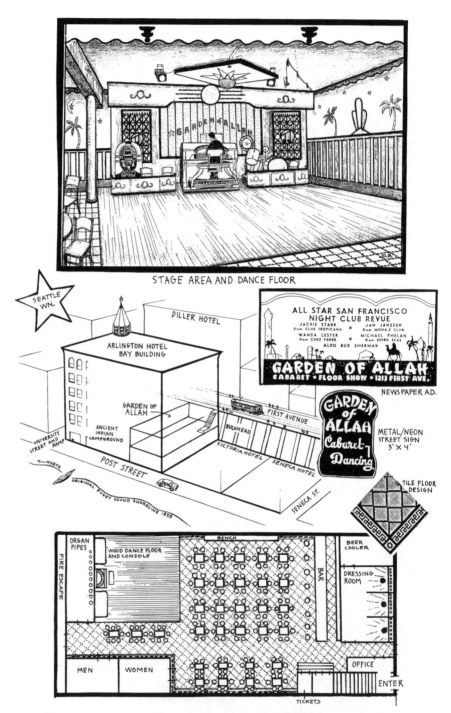

STAGE AREA AND DANCE FLOOR

★ These drawings show the floor plan of the Garden of Allah cabaret and the view from the front tables of the organ and stage at the opening of a show. (Drawings by Don Paulson)

★ Ad for the Garden of Allah.

class men revealed in other ways that their relationships had been transformative. Female impersonators were known for defying the role stereotypes. They usually took the role of "top" or active partner in sex, ran the households, and made the decisions.*

The postwar gay and lesbian cultures were in ferment, the sort of yeast to make an instant success of a new nightspot catering to their self-awareness. The Garden was the perfect place to look at being gay or lesbian through the gender-bending, gay-affirming performances on the stage. This was to be a critical chapter in the history of American gays and lesbians "coming out" into the greater society.

"Coming out" didn't yet mean acknowledging a lesbian or gay identity to oneself and within protective social settings; in the 1930s the phrase sometimes referred to one's first sexual experience, but often it meant one had been introduced to the gay world. George Chauncey found the 1930s meaning of the term rooted in enormous drag balls held in New York, Chicago, and other cities; reflecting high society, "coming out" referred to the introduction of a new "debutante" into gay society.* Although there had been gay and lesbian bars in big coastal cities in the 1930s, after the war new bars opened and flourished in cities all over the country, providing sanctuaries—at least for those who managed to miss the police raids. (Seattle police raided gay bars rarely; I know of only a couple of raids, both in the 1950s.) With both con-

*Ki-ki women, Faderman said, were "those who would not choose a role." Faderman, p. 168.

*Chauncey, *Gay New York; Gender, Urban Culture, and the Making of the Gay Male World 1890–1940* (New York: Basic Books, 1994), pp. 7–8; Bérubé, p. 6.

fidence and fear, lesbians and gays gathered in the Garden of Allah in Seattle and new places like it in other cities for fun, conversation, romance, and overtures to sex. (For many, of course, even "coming out" in places like the Garden seemed far too dangerous. Only the drags and butches displayed their identities openly, and drags especially risked arrest under ordinances used to harass cross-dressers.)

The reluctance to own up to one's gay identity was to be a brake on the movement for gay and lesbian recognition throughout the century. But by 1946, many men and women strove to live their lives honestly. Those decisions spurred many to examine the place of lesbians and gay men in postwar America. Their answers led many into a deeper awareness of being gay; others came to realize that their identity was, and would long remain, a battlefield in the nation's politics. The Garden of Allah was shaping the consciousness of Seattle gays in the same years as the earliest modern gay-political groups were being formed in America.

The Mattachine Society was founded in Los Angeles in 1951 with leadership by gay men who were influenced by the Communist Party and wanted to foster a sense of pride and achievement among homosexuals, and to inspire gays to drop what Harry Hay, one of the cofounders, calls "hetero-imitative" behavior.* The first national lesbian group, The Daughters of Bilitis, was formed in 1955, at first to promote social opportunities, but later to cooperate with Mattachine and other gay groups in advancing political interests. By the mid-1960s, both groups were torn apart by fights between cautious members and militants who were willing to directly confront, and if necessary demonstrate against, gay oppression. By the end of the 1960s, however, lesbians and gay men were engaging in direct political action, not to mention street confrontations such as the Stonewall Rebellion in New York City in 1969. By 1969, in New York and Seattle, gays and lesbians were a force to be recognized, but in 1946, they still had much to learn. The patrons and performers at the Garden and all the early gay bars were the assembling troops, acquiring the consciousness that would clear the way for Stonewall.

BACK TO THE GARDEN OF ALLAH

After the Garden's eager first-nighters paid their dollars at the bottom of the stairway from First Avenue, they opened the door to a blast of sound: the roar of the Wurlitzer theater pipe organ, the noisy crowd, and sounds of the bar. After customers passed an off-duty police officer and a woman hired by the police for such duty, both of whom were there to see that two same-sex patrons didn't touch each other, they stepped down three more steps to the tiled floor of the Garden. As many as two hundred people might crowd into the low-ceilinged, 50-by-100-ft. room.

The tables near the stage filled with the gay crowd, but since the Garden's owners paid off the police, tourists and straight Seattle residents were encouraged to come in

---

*Stuart Timmons, *The Trouble With Harry Hay; Founder of the Modern Gay Movement* (Boston: Alyson Publications, 1990).

as well. The bar in the back of the room kept up a steady flow of beer, wine, and champagne. The tourist and slumming crowd took to the Garden of Allah partly because of its risqué atmosphere, and because they could observe cross-dressing from a safe distance, and partly because straights and gays could mix and even learn about each other with no strings attached. Jeff Court remembered overhearing a heated argument between his parents who had just been to the Garden of Allah. "Mom said the fairies were the men and the dykes were the women, but Dad insisted the women were the fairies and the men were the dykes." The Garden offered tourists just enough anonymity and formality that they could feel safe.

When the Wurlitzer roared its overture and the light fell on the emcee tossing off lines, all laden with the double meanings that both black performers and female impersonators had learned to use in defiance of straight, white social conventions, the audience found itself observing theater rich in tradition. The star impersonators at the Garden, all gay, were thoroughly professional entertainers, talented and dedicated to perfecting their acts. They were the last generation of professional men who played the stage personas of women to the fullest from dress and movement to the singing voice. The impersonators were supported by a cast of both gay and straight entertainers from the dying vaudeville circuit—musicians, jugglers, comedians, singers, and even a dog act. (No one has told me of a bona fide male impersonator who performed at the Garden of Allah. Theater historians say that the male impersonators, who evolved from the cross-dressed role of "principal boy" in British pantomime, virtually disappeared in America by the 1930s.)

The Garden's impersonators performed two classic minstrel-show characters, the Prima Donna and the Dame, transformed by generations of actors and changing modes of theatrical presentation. The Prima Donna had evolved from the character of the tragic "yellow girl," a woman suspended between slavery and the demands of white masters. The character was an elegant chanteuse, a women of quality who was unable to hide the tragedy of being a social outcast. The Dame, played out in a variety of "funny old gal" roles, such as gossips or frumpy housewives, made women the butt of crude comedy just as the earliest minstrel shows had made dark-skinned black women objects of ridicule.*

The Prima Donnas at the Garden went well beyond the role of elegant chanteuse, however, in practicing the art of the striptease. Burlesque theater had added the strip, an erotic element with a subversive twist, in the late 1920s. Gay eroticism came out in the open even in the homage to the older forms of female impersonation and the burlesque striptease and it had the same serious motivation as straight eroticism: sex. Lesbians cheered the Prima Donnas at the Garden with as much enthusiasm as did the gay men, but they spoke about enjoying the artistry of the performance, noting the costumes and makeup and the talent reflected in the routine—in short, they checked the illusion to see if the performance was convincing. The gay men in the audience

*A recent study of minstrelsy also examines homoerotic aspects of the performances. Eric Lott, *Love and Theft: Blackface Minstrelsy and the American Working Class* (New York: Oxford University Press, 1993).

★ Jackie Starr was noted for his striptease. This picture was taken when the touring Jewel Box Revue played Seattle in 1939.

checked the illusion, too, but they also responded to the eroticism of a man stripping before them.

The strip was a powerful connection between the impersonators and those in the audience. Most people are fascinated with the naked body, and tantalized by the prospect of seeing one. Lesbians and gay men appreciated the messages in nudity without being overcome by the social messages about perversion. Gay men, because of oppression, were coming to exalt sexuality as an essential part of their identity. The messages of the strip were that there was humor in sex, that being sexual was fun and natural, that it pushed the limits of community tolerance, and that the impersonators had the courage to use art to push those limits. The strip, at least for men, encoded vital messages of gay culture.

The shows at the Garden of Allah were dominated by acts and characters in the burlesque tradition, caricatures in song, dance, and costume. Hotcha Hinton personified the burlesque influence more than anyone else. Indeed, she may have created a type all her own. She wasn't a Prima Donna, but she wouldn't play the Dame role with its abrasive ridicule of women, either. Camp, the theatrical humor of the impersonator, found its home in Hotcha. She thrived on what Esther Newton has called its main ingredient—incongruity.*

Jackie Starr and Francis Blair were the premier Prima Donnas, the entertainers all other acts supported. Like other impersonators of the day, they had learned their craft on vaudeville and burlesque stages. They also stripped, but as with all Prima Donnas the act had to be elegant and sophisticated. Other impersonators also played Prima Donnas and some like Lee Leonard merged or alternated the Prima Donna and Dame roles. Starr occasionally played the Dame, or "funny old gal," as did Kenny Bee and Blair. Bee and Blair carried the Dame role at the Garden; their best-known roles were Two Old Bags from Tacoma. (At the famous San Francisco drag club Finocchio's, the same kind of routine was called Two Old Bags from Oakland. In New York, it was Hoboken. Every city thrives on the ridicule of a presumed inferior counterpart.)

Certainly, the artistry of those female impersonators connected with audiences, touched them with humor and pathos. People remember the enthusiastic audiences, the cheering and shouting for the performers. The energy of the experience strengthened the bonds that united the members of the audience. All were aware that while the artists might be appreciated in the safe haven of the Garden at night, they could be harassed the next morning on the city's streets. Such people, forced to the margins of the community, ignited a special empathy in other people who know the same experience. Bound by common histories of fear, prejudice, and aspiration, impersonators and gay men and women could read between the lines of the songs and routines and identify with the exaggerated emotions presented on the stage. The very acts of performing and watching were outlawed in many cities in America. Best of all, the impersonators knew how to laugh at themselves, to see humor in tragic circumstances that were all too familiar to lesbians and gays, and they aroused their audiences to face their lives with the same sense of whimsy and optimism. The theatrical energy of female impersonators is extremely strong, unlike any other stage sexuality.

*Esther Newton, *Mother Camp: Female Impersonators in America* (Chicago: University of Chicago Press, 1972), p. 106. See also Kennedy and Davis, p. 383.

There was a deeper source of empathy as well. Men dressed as women signified the dual sexuality of human beings, the pull of things masculine and things feminine in every individual. Every performance offered many layers of sexual meaning: androgynous men and women, cross-dressing, stripping. The art of the impersonators' performances, whatever the literal meanings of the words, must have catalyzed or threatened latent feelings of sexual identity.

In these closing paragraphs, I want to explain what I believe is most important about the history of the Garden of Allah. An important legacy of the Garden of Allah is that Seattle lesbians and gays enjoyed the freedom to assemble without police harassment. On the street, gays and lesbians took their chances, to be sure, but in the Garden the police department counted its money and smiled benignly, if unwittingly, on the birth of a gay community.

As they watched the Prima Donnas and the Dames, lesbians and gays were forming, bit by bit, a community of interests, experiences, and hopes. Each table conversation conveyed word by word a sense of shared identity and a style of coping with its fears and pleasures. Each song or dance communicated not only an attitude toward life, but between the lines a coded message that others shared the same life. Any evening at the Garden of Allah offered simultaneously great traditions of theater, continuous reminders of the repressiveness of American society toward its marginal members, and powerful models for opposing that prejudice.

Every performer and patron that I talked to spoke about remembering his or her enthusiasm for the Garden of Allah. I believe that what they remember as enthusiasm for the cabaret is a great deal like the euphoria that accompanies a new-found freedom, the unrestrained exuberance that marks one who is coming out. In that rush of energy, a self-proclaiming gay man or lesbian suddenly becomes open to all the possibilities of existence from sexuality and friendship to political action. This is what I believe to be the profound legacy of the Garden of Allah: it validated gay existence for a generation that had survived a depression and a world war, giving lesbians and gays the pride and energy to invent protective and affirmative institutions in a hostile society.

It would be foolhardy to argue that a cabaret alone gave birth to a city's gay liberation movement. The evidence suggests, however, that it was an incubator for the lesbian and gay consciousness that later would yield true leaders of the movement and ready followers for the first daring forays into the public arena. Seattle provided a unique stage for the birth of a gay community. In the framework of a police-enforced protection for establishments like the Garden of Allah, gay consciousness was allowed to grow unhindered. A culture of pride was shared by female impersonators and by their lesbian and gay fans. Both patrons and impersonators testified about the positive character of their experience. While time may have softened memories of harsh times, there was little suggestion in interviews with patrons and performers of the sense of stigma and moral downfall sensed by Esther Newton in her study of female impersonators in Chicago and Kansas City in the 1960s.

The oppression of homosexuals took a heavy toll in Seattle then as it does now. Gays and lesbians paid for society's hatred with their lives and dignity. Yet the Garden's story contradicts the common wisdom that drag and gay bars only fed on the self-hatred of their patrons and performers. One has to remember that a decade after the closing of the Garden of Allah, drag artists were losing hope. Impersonators no longer sang or danced, but merely mimed to recordings by popular singers. It was also a time of confusion and distrust not yet focused by the first efforts at gay activism and the first city ordinances ending repressive laws against gays and lesbians.

In the postwar years, in the Garden of Allah, the Seattle gay and lesbian community stepped downstage. No longer hidden behind the sets or writing the lines for the stars, gays were the stars in their own club. The Garden was the oasis that appeared mysteriously out of a searing desert of conformity and bigotry.

chapter I

VILMA: SEATTLE IN THE THIRTIES

★

Vilma had been in Seattle since 1930 and was one of the city's best known gay men. His hangout for all that time was the Double Header, a tavern where he worked on weekends until his last illness. He died in early 1993 at the age of eighty-one. We talked about his life as a gay man—"queen" or "fairy"—in Pioneer Square in the 1930s, but he died before we could begin to talk about the Garden. (The Pioneer Square district begins five blocks south of the site of the Garden of Allah; the square itself is marked by a Victorian pergola and an Alaskan native totem pole. The Double Header is nearby.)

★

I was born in Minneapolis on April 13, 1912. We Aries are leaders of men but all I ever wanted to do is have fun and that has come true. I had a pretty good childhood and I was treated well by everyone in my family. I think they accepted me as different right from the start. I was a good uncle. A couple of straight nephews followed me out west to be near me.

I've never had any hangups about being gay. I've always been myself and I never had any religious hangups, thank God. A gay friend of mine turned religious and he blamed himself all his life.

I came out sexually when I was twelve years old. He was this darling sixteen-year-old neighborhood boy that I was in love with since age nine. We'd sneak down to our basement to make love on a tall pile of old mattresses. No one ever found out. There wasn't any hangup about it for either of us—we loved it! To us it was the natural thing. I never felt I was doing anything wrong ever.

I never actually came out to anyone in my family; you did not do that in those days. I guess I felt if I didn't speak the words they wouldn't be forced to deal with it and could let it go. But my mother began to suspect when I started going in drag at fifteen. At first I was going to a "costume ball." After a few more times she stopped asking.

That was when I bought my first dress. My best friend Red and

★ This pergola has marked Seattle's Pioneer Square since the turn of the century. Restrooms were below the pergola. The 614 Tavern and the Palm Theatre were in the block of buildings at the rear. The totem pole is behind the streetcar. (Photo courtesy of Special Collections Division, University of Washington Libraries)

I went into this thrift store and I saw this beautiful blue satin gown but it had the $10 blue tag on it. I didn't have the money so while Red was busy with the saleslady I switched the blue tag to a $3 green tag. I asked her how much the dress was and she said $3. "Oooooh," I said, "I'll take it."

Mother always wore Cuban heels. I said to her one day, "Come over to the store with me because I want to buy a pair of high heels with three-inch spikes." I picked out a black pair and I asked my mother to try them on. She said, "Try them on your-self. They're for you, not for me." The saleslady looked strangely at me and my mother said, "Oh, he's going to dress up as a girl and go to a costume ball." The saleslady said, "Why, that's a wonderful idea."

In 1927 I knew eight kids who dressed in drag, but we called it female imperson-ation then. Minneapolis was big enough that we could blend in but we had to be care-ful. Red and I went to this old-fashioned dance place where they wouldn't let us in. "Come back in a couple years," they said. So Red and I went home and got in drag and went back and they let us right in. They didn't even recognize us and we got to dance with all the boys. One time eight of us went down there in drag. Nobody caught on and we had a ball.

I never saw any old drags that I recognized on the street. They were on the vaudeville circuits and at carnivals you'd see a drag or two in the girlie show and the half-woman, half-man act.

One night I went to a vaudeville show at the Palace Theatre in Minneapolis and there were a man and a woman on the show billed as "The Beauty and the Beast." She was very beautiful and he was made up very sinister. Later, I was standing in front of the theater and this man picked me up and took me to his hotel room. I found out it was the beast and he sure was a handsome beast. I was sixteen. I also saw two brothers, West and West, in comedy drag that night. They were very funny. I went home and told my mother she should go see them but she had no money so I went out and sold my body and bought two tickets and took my mother to the show. She thought West and West were grand.

Two friends of mine, Dorothy Dalton and Gary Foss, visited Seattle and raved about it. That's all I heard, Seattle, Seattle, Seattle and this fabulous place called the Casino and all the neat kids there. One day I met my mother on the street and when we parted I kissed her and said, "I'll see you later." Then I went downtown and happened to meet Gary Foss who said, "Let's go to Seattle," and on a whim I said yes. So we hopped on a boxcar right then and headed west.

We arrived in Seattle on June 15, 1930, and headed straight for the Casino. Two men on the street looked us over and one of them said to the other, "Oh, oh, new competition in town." We learned later they were two detectives from the police vice department. They kept their eye on all the queens and hustlers in town but they were okay. They were fair.

The Casino was in the basement below the Double Header. We could hardly wait to get down those stairs. It was a large basement without any decoration except a few signs for Coca Cola and Pepsi Cola and later when Franklin Roosevelt became president the managers, John and Margaret Delevitti, put up a picture of FDR which is still there today.

When you came down the stairs from Washington Street, you'd find a small restaurant area and a long bar across the room where they sold soft drinks and near beer, which was one-half percent alcohol, the legal limit during Prohibition. But we'd go down to a shacktown called Hooverville and buy a pint of whiskey and bring it back to the Casino and drink it there at the bar. A lot of places let you bring your own bottle of booze as long as you kept it hidden. The Casino had two pool tables and tables for playing cards. It was a crossroads. There were lots of gay kids at the Casino and we made friends right away.

Pioneer Square was where the gay kids hung out in 1930. A number of places let the queens in—restaurants, pool halls, and speakeasies. After Prohibition a few taverns let us in. I met my boyfriend at the Ocean tavern and we lived together for thirteen years. Then he got married and they had two kids and I became an uncle but they never knew their father and I were lovers. There was a pool hall across the street from the Casino where all the boosters [shoplifters] and hustlers hung out. John and Margaret wouldn't let anyone mess with the queens. A queen was anyone who was gay and didn't try to hide it. They protected us and we loved them for that, but you didn't mess with them or take advantage of their kindness. They'd do anything for you if they liked you, even bail you out of jail, but if you crossed John he'd throw you out in a minute, gay or straight. The Casino was the only place on the West Coast that was so open and free for gay people. But John paid off the police; he was good at working the payoff system.

Pioneer Square was still pretty nice in the 1930s, not like the '50s and '60s when it really went downhill. There would be people filling the sidewalks twenty-four hours a day. It was the poor part of town, but it was where all the action was. There were lots of restaurants. Hamburger steak was 10 cents and a bowl of chili with all the bread you could eat was also 10 cents.

Lots of gay kids went to the burlesque theaters—the State, Rialto, and the Palm— especially when female impersonators were on the bill. The theaters wouldn't tell the public which dancers were female impersonators. We were friends with all the girls at the burlesque houses. They'd come down to the Casino or we'd party with them at a speakeasy or an after-hours club. For some reason they just loved the queens. The Palm Burlesque Theatre's last show was at 3 a.m. and we'd go there to cruise and either meet someone for a good time or make some money—preferably the latter. Those were depression days. You had to walk that extra mile.

We had nicknames for ourselves. There was me, Vilma, after the actress Vilma Banky. And Chicago Marge, Fay, Violet, Maggie, Huntington, Peaches, Midnight Rose, Filipino Alice, Sally Thurston, Myrna Loy, Boston Nell, Dora Waite, Countess Dee Dee, Mexican Lil, Wilhelmina, Mary Ann, Mother Blondie, Christine, Clea, Rene, Frisco, Ginny, Miss Whigham, Hanna Banana, and Madame Fingers Drag (she had two thumbs on one hand). Although we had the girls' names, most of us weren't drag queens.

I never saw any Indian queens until the 1940s, but there were black and Filipino and Mexican queens.[*] I still know a black queen. Her name is Alex but she doesn't get around much anymore because her legs are bothering her. When we get together people think we're a couple of giggling schoolgirls.

Wilhelmina was a nice kid, still going to high school in 1933. I remember when she first came out; she was so scared. She came down the stairs to the Casino and paused on the landing trying to look pretty and someone spoke to her and she fled up the stairs. Five minutes later she got nerve enough to come down the stairs only to fly up the stairs again. When she came down the stairs again someone just grabbed her and said, "It's okay, honey," and took her by the hand and introduced her to all the kids. Wilhelmina came out.

---

[*]Early settlers in Washington territory noted at least two Indian women who dressed as men. Men who dressed as women were identified by Puget Sound Indians by the words "tcha kai dai." Interview with David Buerge, 1994.

Hanna Banana was a darling old queen who lived in and out of drag all her life. She was still doing drag in her nineties when she died in her Pioneer Square hotel room. She'd been around Seattle since the Alaska Gold Rush days and said Seattle was always a ball. She said Seattle was always a hot town for gay people because of all the single men that traveled through. Seattle was a party town and she said she gave "many a poor traveler food, shelter, and the comfort of a warm cheek." Hanna was as wild as a March hare but a real sweetheart. She'd come down to the Casino and all the gay kids would treat her like royalty and she'd listen to all their troubles and offer advice and camp it up and tell wild stories about her life. She was into lumberjacks. Oh, how she loved her lumberjacks.

It was great back in the 1930s, but the queens have changed just like everything else. We were all queens then. You knew who you were. I'd see them waving off the boxcars; you could tell them, you still can. I have no patience with gays who pretend to be straight. You can tell by the way they hold their cigarette, or eat, or anything. They're just queens like we are. You don't have to throw them in your lap to know they're queens. On the other hand, there's nothing wimpy about a drag queen.*

Once some guy made a smart remark to Miss Antoinette, a black female impersonator, at the Six-Eleven tavern. She picked up her purse and whacked him alongside his head, knocked him off his chair, and sat on him. "Sweetheart," she said, "You'd better shut your mouth before I get mad."

Back then it was like kids together, fellows, comrades. We'd all go out and make whatever money we could and always ask a friend, "Did you eat today?" If they hadn't, you'd say, "Well, I made some money today, come on, let's go get something to eat." Everyone was friendlier then; none of this, "I'm better off than you are!" The gay kids looked out for each other. We had to. We had to protect ourselves. Lots of people were killed for being gay. A friend of mine was killed by two sailors in a hotel above the Garden of Allah. He wouldn't hurt anybody but he was the one who had to die.

I was washing dishes for awhile so I had money to rent a hotel room with my lover Red. But later we'd hear these faint taps on the door from friends who needed a place to stay. Sometimes we'd be four in the bed, three at the foot of the bed on the floor, and three at the side of the bed on the floor.

Once in Chicago Gita Gilmore, a female impersonator, snubbed me on the street but later that night I heard this faint tap on the door and there she was. I said, "Come on in, Gita." That was before she was famous but after she became famous she was

---

*Stephen Blair told me: "I've known some tough drag queens: Choo Choo Laverne, Overcoat Charlie, Black Orchid, and another black queen, Dinge Dixie (who named himself), and Stepladder Kate, who was a very short but feisty drag performer who brought a stepladder on stage with her. [A dinge queen was a white man who preferred black men.] Black Orchid was so strong she could pick up her trick with one hand. She was only five feet tall and four and a half feet of that was cock. Let me tell you those queens were tough. They could fistfight and nobody messed with them."

always good to me. One day in Chicago in 1938 someone knocked on my door. I was going with this guy who was being tailed by the FBI on marijuana charges. I was in a red kimono with fluffy slippers and makeup when I opened the door to the two FBI men. They didn't blink an eye as they'd seen everything before.

There wasn't a lot of fagbashing in those days but there was always someone out there to hassle any gay kid. A couple rough types came on to Gary Foss and got twenty-five cents from him so they thought, "Oh, this is easy, we'll do this to all the queens." They tried to get money from me but I ran away and at the doorway of the Casino I saw the two detectives who made that remark about "more competition in town." I told them about the two guys who just tried to take my rent money. The detectives went after the two and asked them, "What do you want to take his money for?" They said, "Oh, he's just a queer." The detectives said, "If he's queer why the hell do you want to take his money for? You'd better get your ass outta here or you know where you'll land." They left and I never saw them again. Sometimes the cops were almost protective of us. But that is not to say that the queens or drag queens were not dragged in, especially if they were hustling in drag. Queens have always been dragged in but a lot of the time they almost asked for it with an attitude of not giving a damn.

The park around the totem pole was the hot cruising place in Seattle. No matter who you were, it was the place to people-watch. They had a beautiful public restroom under the pergola that the black shoeshine man kept spotless. Across from the restroom, we used to sit on the railing above the Pittsburgh cafeteria in the basement of the Pioneer building. They'd ask us not to sit there; I guess they didn't think their customers wanted to look up at a bunch of queens' asses hanging over the edge. Eventually they put spikes on the railings, but we sat there anyway. We had a perfect view of the restroom. The city used to advertise that it was the "finest public restroom west of the Mississippi."

We also went to the Turkish Baths around Pioneer Square. There were lots of single men traveling through Seattle and bathhouses catered to their needs. I usually went to the Morrison Hotel Turkish Baths or the South End Baths. They were a mix of gay and straight. If you were actively gay then the bathhouses were hot. The bathhouse in the old Seattle Hotel didn't allow queens.

The totem pole in Pioneer Square was stolen from an Indian site in Alaska. One late night it burned down and I got blamed for it. Just because I hung out there they thought I did it but I was in Minneapolis at the time so I was let off the hook. A bunch of tramps were sitting next to it and had a little fire going and the totem pole caught fire by accident. But who did they blame? The queens, of course. Then the city commissioned the same tribe to carve another one and sent them $5,000 to do it. They wrote back and said, "Thanks for the $5,000. That pays for the first one that you stole 50 years ago and it'll cost you another $5,000 for a new one." So the Indians got the last laugh and we got a new totem pole for $10,000.

In the early 1930s, I met a kid from Yakima by the name of Bill York at the Casino and we fell in love and rented a room for seventy-five cents a night at the old Grand

Union Hotel at Fifth and Yesler. But true love never lasts more than two and a half weeks so my buddy Gary Foss and I decided to go to San Francisco. That's when San Francisco was "good" but we met an old timer down there who said the Barbary Coast days was when San Francisco was good!

We caught a ferry to Tacoma for twenty-five cents and hopped a boxcar to San Francisco. A lot of queens traveled by boxcar in those depression years. There was no money to do anything but make out the best you could. Some of the Seattle queens would bunch up and travel to San Francisco on boxcars and stay for three or four months. Then the queens in San Francisco would come up and stay in Seattle for three or four months, so when they all returned to whichever city they'd be "new" in town. Sometimes we'd meet each other in between the cities on the rails. That was a wild time, lots of hot stories and carrying on and we shared our food over a campfire along the tracks. We covered ourselves with newspapers at night. We traveled the rails as males but I heard about queens who traveled the rails in drag.

I never saw many drags on the street in the early 1930s—lots of them on Halloween and New Year's—but Chicago Marge was always in drag and even hustled in drag. One evening a mean cop we called Mother Sherry, who hated drag queens, overheard two queens talking about Chicago Marge being in drag that night. Mother Sherry went out looking for her on his beat from Madison Street to Pioneer Square. When he spotted her, Chicago Marge dashed into the Florence Theatre [now the Pioneer Square Theatre] and sat in the women's section. He walked up and down the aisles looking for her. When she left he spotted her again and chased her up the alley behind the theater but she got away.

Apparently someone from the *Star* newspaper saw this and in the next day's edition there was a cartoon of Marge running up the alley with her long dress pulled up and showing masculine calves with Mother Sherry chasing her—cops wasting time and money. Mother Red was another mean cop. We'd see him coming and we'd cross the street to another cop's beat. When Mother Red left we'd go back to the totem pole and cruise again.

The cops of the '30s were mostly pretty good to the queens as long as you didn't push things, then they could be real mean and you could get hurt. They were paid off so that kept a lid on things. They could give you a bad time if they were in the mood and they also liked to play around with you.

In 1935, I had one cop get me up against a wall in the alley behind the Double Header and play with my tits. Just then my boyfriend walked by. He didn't know I was a hustler and I thought he'd catch on but he saw that it was a cop and that he was hassling me so he walked on. I finally told the cop, "If you keep on playing with my tits it'll cost you." I never had anything to do with cops but I knew gay kids that did. A friend of mine used to give this cop blow jobs on a regular basis. There was a lot of backroom activity in those days, cops getting special favors from business people and others.

Then there were these two cops who used to pick me and Mother Blondie up in a squad car and take us over to a whorehouse in Chinatown and say they were going to make us fuck the girls there. We said we didn't want to fuck the girls but they'd take us there anyway. As soon as they'd go in, we'd run back to the Casino. Those damn guys did that two or three times a month for awhile.

But they were very lenient to the gay kids. They were good cops but they liked to fuck around with us. I'm sure they got a good laugh out of that at the police station.

In 1939, Mother Blondie, Mary Ann, and four other queens were sentenced to the work farm in Georgetown for ninety days. They met Filipino Alice there; she was a "turn-trick." Those kids had a wild time out there with the other guys. They'd drape a blanket around the bunk bed at night and use it for sex purposes. Finally the guards went to the court judge and said, "If you don't get those cocksuckers out of there we're going to quit. They fuck all night, sleep all day, and don't want to work!" The judge let them go in half the time.

Filipino Alice used to play pool at the Casino. She was a sharp pool player. She'd be playing these different guys for fun or money and eventually she'd say, "Do you want to spend a few extra dollars at my place?"

Then there was Christine, who was always in the old jail up on Yesler. One day they sent her down to the lobby and told her to mop the floor. They wanted to get rid of her. They set it up for her to escape but she didn't want to leave. After she mopped the floor she went back upstairs to the jail. Once Christine picked up a trick and took him up to her hotel room. But they were followed by two cops who peeked through the keyhole until they were finished and then arrested them. When the judge heard the story he was so mad at the cops he threw it out of court.

There was this kid Miss Whigham—he lived in the old Cascade Hotel—who got arrested for turning tricks. She kept this little book that noted her tricks day by day—how much she made, if the guy was clean, etc. When they arrested her they took the little book with them and handed it to the judge. He was Judge Gordon, but we called him Kitty Gordon. He was a good judge and was lenient on the queens. The judge looked through the little book and said, "Well, it looks like you didn't do too good on Thursday. If I let you go what will you do?" The judge wanted him to say, "I'll leave town," but the kid said, "Well, I guess I'll go home and go to bed." The judge let him go and the queen went home and went to bed.

There was a lot of marijuana in the '30s; you just had to know the right people. Then they outlawed it and it became very dangerous to have it. When liquor became legal all of a sudden marijuana became the big evil. For ten cents you could buy a "finger stick" which is a fat joint. For $2 you could buy two Prince Albert tobacco cans of it. They liked to use tobacco cans for concealment.

One night we all got together—Clea, Rene, Frisco, Ginny, and Madame Fingers Drag. After awhile others dropped by and soon we had a party going. Marijuana had just become illegal and we had a six-inch pyramid pile of it on the table when the police came to the door after someone complained about the noise. I apologized and said we were having a book party and that I'd keep the noise down. Thank God they didn't see the pile of marijuana, which would have meant years in prison.

Above the Casino was the Double Header tavern which was a dance hall during Prohibition. They had a dance band every night—piano, drums, and a horn. Women could dance with other women but men could not dance with men. After Prohibition ended John and Margaret managed the Double Header as a straight tavern. They welcomed the gay kids but the DH was the domain of the B-girls. The Double Header was a swinging place, a real mix of everyone, just like it is today. The Casino was the gay hangout all through the '30s, but the gay kids would come up from the Casino around closing time and if the men didn't make out with one of the ladies some of them would settle for a gay kid. The men would justify it by saying, "A hole's a hole, even if it's on a jackass."

Around 1946 the queens ran the B-girls out of the Double Header and it became the gay hangout. The Garden of Allah opened at the same time and we all started going up there to see the shows.

chapter 2

THE MEN: "LET'S GO TO THE GARDEN"
★

In this and the next chapter, Seattle men and women recall what it was like to be part of the Garden crowd—the house staff and the regular patrons who commanded the best seats and noisily adored the cast members. While these interviews recapture the joys of the Garden, they also reveal the pains and fears of young gay men and lesbians who were finding their gay identities at the end of World War II. In the following interviews, Seattle men describe how the cabaret became central to their social lives.

BILL PARKIN

Bill Parkin has shared his home in Seattle's Capitol Hill neighborhood with at least one hundred friends in the past thirty years. Until he recently left a job as a bookkeeper for a bar, he had been in the gay-bar business all his adult life. In his early sixties, Parkin bowls in a gay league and has a long row of trophies. Parkin took me inside the Garden and onto its stage at showtime.

★

First Avenue was a mecca for young people, a place where you learned about the other things in life. From upper Pike Street to Pioneer Square, First Avenue was a sea of sailors. It was twenty blocks of honky-tonk taverns, restaurants, all-night theaters, pawn shops, army surplus stores, cheap hotels, and peep shows. Many parents forbade their children to hang out there but for some of us it was our secret place. It was the hot spot and gay people always know where the hot spots are.

My buddy Tommy knew Thelma, the police matron at the Garden of Allah. With fake ID that I bought on First Avenue from a man who also sold pornography under the counter, I got in and became a steady patron.

You had no illusions about the Garden of Allah. The Garden was very earthy, a real underground decadent cabaret straight out of Toulouse Lautrec and you loved it. It was daring and romantic and a

★ Bill Parkin
owned the Pike
Street Tavern, a gay
business, in the
1960s.

place where you expected to have fun. For gays, and straights who could appreciate a more basic atmosphere, it was "our place."

A dark Victorian wainscoting ran around the room and palm trees and stars were stenciled on the wall which gave it a certain Casbah atmosphere. The space was low light and could be a little cold in winter. The tables were tacky and the chairs scrapy and so close together you could move your chair a little and be at another table. There were dark blue and pink fluorescent-type bulbs behind sconces so the Garden was filled with a soft, subdued light—very, very seductive. That's the only way it looked

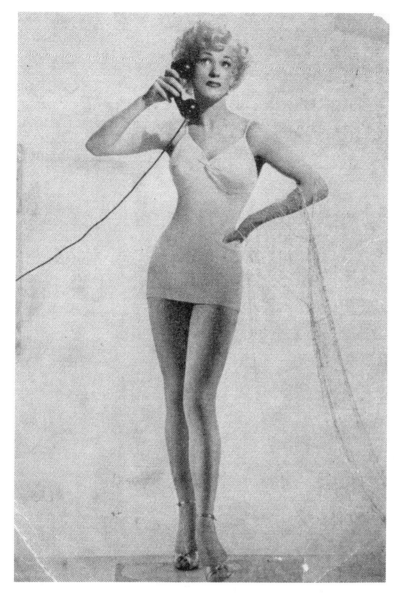

★ Billy DeVoe, the "Park Avenue Hillbilly" (after Dorothy Shay), belted out upbeat songs. As emcee, DeVoe teased his audience with broad sexual humor that sometimes confused them but more often was accepted warmly. He retired from impersonation in 1983 after thirty-five years of performing as a Prima Donna in major clubs around the country. "It wasn't all a drag," he said. "In fact, it was wonderful. Use my real name, Joe Dusin. I've always been proud of my career and of who I am."

good because there were no fancy furnishings (except the beautiful Wurlitzer pipe organ). But the atmosphere was captivating. You never noticed the beer or cigarette butts spilled on the floor or an occasional whiff of urine from the old bathrooms. You'd be too engrossed in the show and fascinated by the repartee of the audience and entertainers.

The stage lighting at the Garden was good for its time with colored spots controlled by a small switchboard. There was a light over the organist and drummer and another over the bar. The microphone hung from a hook in the ceiling at center stage

★ Jackie Starr stayed close to the Garden mike when he sang; a slight turn away and his voice would fade out.

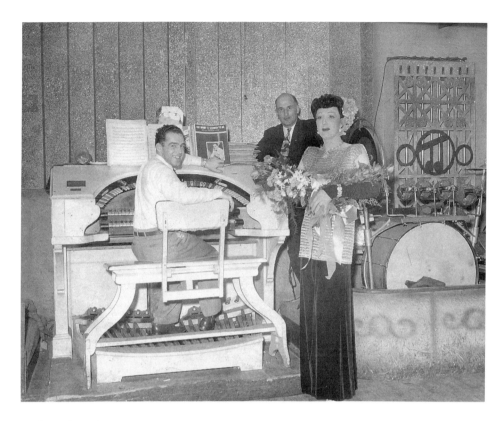

★ The Wurlitzer theater organ accompanied every show. Jackie Starr accepted bouquets and applause at the end of a 1948 engagement while Jimmy Baker, the organist, and Earl Steves, the drummer, watched. The sheet music for Jackie's closing number was "Oh! What It Seemed to Be."

and could be raised up or down. Countess Estelle said you had to keep it right in front of your face because if you turned your head you'd lose volume.

There were two shows a night on weekdays and three shows on Fridays and Saturdays. It was closed on Sunday. The show would last forty-five minutes to an hour. The Garden opened at 5 o'clock and closed at midnight. The cover was $1 and a glass of beer was 25 cents. At that time you could still buy a "nickel beer," a small glass of beer for 5 cents. A loganberry flip, which was wine with a splash of 7-Up with ice, cost 25 cents. It was like drinking raspberry pop. I never liked beer so I sat there and drank those bloody things 'til I made myself half sick.

The show would begin with a special number on the pipe organ and Wanda Lester Brown and female impersonator Billy DeVoe often shared the emcee duties. They might begin the show with a vocal—often by Wanda who was a professional jazz and blues singer. They might follow that with a strip, then a comedy act, then a group

★ "Cowgirls" was a popular finale at the Garden. Here, from left, Billy DeVoe, Robin Raye, Jackie Starr, and Hotcha Hinton, reach for their empty holsters.

revue like "Cowgirls" while the organist played a western tune. Then another vocal, etc. It was always a lively show but it had love songs, too, such as "As Time Goes By" sung by Jackie Starr. Wanda and Billy would do patter between the acts while the kids were back changing costumes.

The finale of the show might be everyone on stage singing, "We don't care, we don't care, we don't care what happens to us. We're happy go lucky..." At the end of the evening you might hear the beer carriers say "motel time" or "suck it up" or "motel spelled backwards is 'letom.'" Or they'd say "Come on, get out of here!" or "We got your money, so get the hell out of here!" Then they'd turn on those six three-hundred watt lights which was the only time the Garden of Allah was well lit.

Wanda Brown was very beautiful. She was married to a well-known black drummer, Vernon Brown. They were well-liked. Wanda always wore the latest dress designs and was one of the first to wear a chignon. She wore her hair pulled back so tight it made her look oriental.

Billy DeVoe was "The Blonde Lana Turner." He always wore those slinky white outfits with the slit up the side and he had gorgeous legs. Billy was called the "Park Avenue Hillbilly" because of his Oklahoma accent. His songs included "Feudin', Fussin', and Fightin'," "Hillbilly Heaven," "Mountain Gal," and "Uncle Fudd." I can always remember his opening line at the Garden: "Good evening, Ladies and Gentlemen and the rest of you. The more you clap the more you see so get off your hands

★ Jackie Starr,
Ricky Reynolds,
and Hotcha Hinton
posed after their
"Happy Go Lucky"
routine.

and stop goosing each other." His close was, "Well, fellows, wine and dine and make merry. If you can't make merry look me up. I'm not cheap but I'm awfully damn reasonable."

Billy might go out in the audience and sit on some sailor's lap and wiggle his false boobs in the poor sailor's face. He would be a little confused but it was all in fun. To tourists this was pretty far out stuff. It was such a mix of gender roles and so "sexual," but it was in such high camp you couldn't be offended—embarrassed maybe, but not offended. The Garden had a lot of burlesque atmosphere. You could get away with things in this controlled environment; of course, they paid off the police.

Once in awhile you'd get a drunk in there yakking off and firing barbs but they were usually shot down because nobody could top those kids. They'd say, "Honey, you open your mouth one more time and I'll put a toilet seat around it and we can all use it." Or they'd say, "Honey, I asked for toilet paper and you come rolling in." They took their lives in their own hands when they tried to match wits with a drag queen! Usually they were shot down politely so there was never any violence.

A lot of military kids would come down to the Garden and Thelma would say, "OK, fellows, come on in, but we don't allow any rough stuff in here."

The music at the Garden was the day's hits and the songs of World War II like "Don't Sit Under the Apple Tree" and "My Bill." Many of the songs had an emphasis on sex because sex was one of the rewards after fighting a war. Sex was one of the ingredients in First Avenue's notorious reputation, gay and straight; it was the cruising place. That carried on into the Korean War because, like World War II, those boys were going off to a foreign land maybe to die. Those nights before sailing was party, party, party. My house looked like the USO. I can remember coming downstairs one morning in my house on Olympic Place and there were twelve Navy neckerchiefs hanging from my frontroom chandelier. There were all these sailors draped all over the sofas and floors and in everyone else's bed but mine!

Between shows at the Garden some people danced to the pipe organ or the gorgeous old juke box with its colored lights and beautiful designs. Mostly people would talk to each other or visit other tables.

Over the years different people organized the shows, but there was a thread of regulars at the Garden like Jackie Starr, Robin Raye, Billy DeVoe, Hotcha Hinton, Wanda Lester Brown, Kenny Bee, Francis Blair, Ricky Reynolds, Jan Jannsen, Skippy LaRue, etc. The show would bring in headliners like Ray Bourbon, Lee Leonard, Bernie Carey, T. C. Jones, and Michael Phalen. They'd stay for four to six weeks. The regulars at the Garden would then get a new show together. That's a terrific amount of work! These kids were the children of vaudeville. They grew up with it. When they got to the Garden of Allah they already knew what to do; they knew how to put together a good variety show with a backup of the pipe organ and a drummer, sometimes a combo.

Jackie Starr was one of the female impersonators that gave the Garden class. When Jackie came on stage the whole place went silent. There was no thought of his gender. On stage he was a lady. Remarkably sophisticated. He wasn't campy but he had a marvelous sense of humor, and always elegant. Jackie was never heckled. Jackie was always very tailored, always the entertainer. In drag he would wear those beautiful suits with the padded shoulders and nice hats—class! Jackie was an illusionist. One sailor said to his buddy, "Look at that broad!" That was common. Jackie was flawless in drag. His voice was almost the same but softer and he never, never went out of character.

It takes a very special talent for a man to pull off a good strip, the right body, the right stage presence. Robin Raye and Jackie Starr were great strippers—they dazzled the audience—they'd strip right down to a G-string and everyone would be shocked.

★ Animal tamer Kenny Bee subdues four wild felines; from left, Billy DeVoe, Jackie Starr, Hotcha Hinton, and Francis Blair, in "Hold That Tiger."

Where were their sexual parts? They had special ways of concealment but it was still hard to believe.

Robin Raye and others joked about calling the female impersonators "Female Im Peter Tasters." Robin was totally insane. He had a voice like an air-raid siren. He was campy and didn't care what people thought, but like Jackie he still had class. For awhile he worked with the dancers at the Rivoli Burlesque Theatre and looked as good as any of the hoofers in the line. Robin was a fabulous stripper. He'd strip right down to a 3-inch by 3-inch G-string. Bobby, as he was called at the Garden, had a big hoo-haw and everybody wondered where in hell he tucked it because it simply wasn't there when he stripped down to a G-string. I asked Billy DeVoe; "Honey," Billy says, "she shoves it up her ass."

Kenny Bee was the house comedian, but he could also sing, act, and was an excellent dancer. In many ways he was a true vaudevillian—he knew how to keep a show going and if anything needed to be done he could do it. Sometimes Kenny would get into drag, but it was always camp drag. His parodies of women, especially frumpy types, would be absolutely hysterical. For instance, he'd have two large rubber balls with handles on them which he'd remove from his brassiere and bounce up and down on the floor like a basketball. He would burlesque women in a way that would just crack everybody up. Of course, one wouldn't do that now as it would be considered very sexist, but this was the 1940s and '50s and the put-down school was rampant then.

The phrase "You will have a happy birthday or you'll answer to sister fuck with your mind!" reminds me of Hotcha Hinton. Vile language! Hotcha would come out on stage and there would be nothing but four letter words, expletives from the time he hit the stage to the time he left the stage. We called Hotcha "garbage mouth." Hotcha was hot, maybe too hot and aggressive, but he was a showman! He could perform through a tornado. Hotcha was a female impersonator Lenny Bruce, years ahead of his time. But Hotcha was a sweetheart—he appeared rough but deep down he was a loving person.

You know, the impersonators often got their lines from women like Anna Russell, Bea Lilly, Sophie Tucker, and Gypsy Rose Lee. But I'd bet that those women first heard some of those lines from the gay kids around them.

Mickey Knight was another female impersonator who was wild. Mickey looked like a southern belle, beautiful lace and hat and a full Scarlett O'Hara ballgown with a white fox stole. Mickey was gorgeous but garbage would come out of his mouth. Mickey would come out on stage trailing that twelve-foot-long white fox stole. She'd say, "What's the difference between a fir and a spruce?" He'd raise his hand and fluff up his hair and say, "That's a spruce." Then he'd snap that fox stole and swirl it around him and say, "This is a fur." He was always playing with that stole. He'd swing it around and hold it like a gigantic penis, making remarks like "This reminds me of who I had last night—it wouldn't stay up either." He didn't have to say anything. His gestures and the expression on his face would send you into hysterics.

Ray Bourbon [Ramon Icarez] was a world-famous female impersonator and played the Garden a lot. He was large and husky and would come out on stage and have that intense aura of a madam or a rich and poised matron—but out would come these visceral lines! One routine was a telephone conversation with a friend where he talks about his trick last night. He'd say, "I threw the trick towel out the window and it dried on the way down and gave a sailor a concussion." His shows were pretty rough, definitely underground material. He got so rough that during the McCarthy era in the 1950s the Seattle Police Department forbade the Garden of Allah to hire him or Lee Leonard because they were "too dirty."

Ray Bourbon traveled in a big Buick convertible like Franklin Roosevelt's. His ex-Marine lover drove, pulling a small travel trailer with about twelve big dogs. The dogs were instrumental in landing him in prison for murder. Bourbon was convicted of masterminding the murder of the keeper of the dogs, who evidently had sold the animals because Bourbon sent little money for their boarding for over three years. He developed leukemia in prison, and died of a heart attack.

Lee Leonard, whose real name was Rubin Elkins, appeared at the Garden and all around Seattle many times and for awhile he and Robin Raye traveled together doing shows. He was one of the oldest persons ever to have a sex change and became Liz Lyons in his 60s. They got rid of that beautiful nine-inch peter and turned it inside out. But that's what he wanted so he had a right to do it.

★ Ray Bourbon, a nationally famous female impersonator, drank a local beer at the Garden. Born near the Texas-Mexican border, he said he's been a borderline case ever since.

Bunny Daniels was a fantastic female impersonator and traveled the country with his own show. He was 6'4" and had that madam look on stage and had worked the Pantages vaudeville circuit in drag. He was good and certainly would have played the Garden but Ray Bourbon and Lee Leonard ganged up on him and said, "If Bunny works the Garden, we'll quit." There was a similarity of acts so it was professional jealousy.

There were always big costume balls on Halloween and New Year's Eve at the Garden. Everyone would show up. The streets of Seattle would be full of people in costume. Anyone who wanted to get in drag could actually appear on the streets without being arrested. It was like Mardi Gras. Even important city people would be downtown—you felt safe because you were behind the mask. People would always make it a point to show up at the Garden during the evening.

The Picture Lady in a sexy dress would take your picture and bring it back developed a while later. The Flower Lady, who was very sweet and looked like a scrubbed

★ Lee Leonard performed on the national circuit and often headlined the Garden bills. In his sixties, after a sex change, he became "The Naughty Liz Lyons," right, and continued to tour.

Apple Annie, would go from bar to bar selling corsages. The Flower Lady came around to all the gay bars for over twenty years. We called her Mother. When Mother would come into the Double Header tavern, Kitty, a flaming redhead queen, would scream, "All right, one of you SOBs buy me a corsage so Mother won't starve tonight!" Someone would cough up the $1.50 for the corsage and pin it on Kitty. The bottom line to this regular routine was that Kitty would then do one of her famous backflips.

There were lots of women at the Garden but everybody noticed the butches. You did not see feminine lesbians then because they looked like everyone else—you saw only the masculine women and feminine men. Everyone was still in the closet. It was too dangerous to be open.

I remember one butch that looked like a Chicago gangster—black pin-striped suit, big tie, cigar, she looked like the Mafia. She was okay, but boy was she tough. If any-one gave her trouble she'd deck 'em. The butches really liked the female imperson-

ators and, in a way, protected them. If anyone ever said a nasty thing to a drag some butch would say, "You got a problem, buddy?" They stuck right out while everyone else was noncommittal.

I became known as Lolly Parkins, the red-headed Elsa Maxwell—hears all, sees all, knows all, tells all. There were parties constantly at my house on Queen Anne Hill.

There were lots of parties in the 1950s. Since the bars closed so early there was nothing to do but have a party. Early in the evening, someone would volunteer to host it. Then the word would go around to the bars where to go and to B.Y.O.B. There were lots of drinks, dancing, and necking at these parties. Nothing was ever stolen; everybody knew everybody else in that core group. There were no drugs at these parties except bennies—we were trained drinkers. Many of us drank a lot in those days but we were expected to behave ourselves and be able to drive home.

People would say, "Let's go out and see Aunt Mary," meaning marijuana. Or they'd say, "Do you want to go bowling?" which meant going to someone's house to smoke marijuana. That was deep underground then; you didn't even use the word marijuana.

Del Greenlee was one of the very few black gay men around in the 1950s. He was the only one I knew. Blacks were not around in the gay community or did not cross the line. Del was liked very much by everybody. What a sweet, fun, and thoughtful man. Del did drag for fun for years. He was a Sagittarius and very outgoing. My bedroom was all white and he was so handsome anyway and with that gorgeous dark body of his. Wow! One night he stayed over with me. Everyone had to take off their shoes when they entered my bedroom and the next morning outside my door and tailing all the way down the long hallway were roller skates, ballet slippers, fluffy slippers, saddle shoes, slip-on penny loafers, rubber boots, etc., all the way down the hall carpet runner. My roommates had put them there.

We were living on the edge. We had just emerged as a community. We had our police payoff system and that gave us a certain amount of protection, but at any moment the police could descend and throw us back into the dark ages. We were very careful about police in those days. We knew they were acting on the attitudes of most people about homosexuals.

One of the benefits from the payoff system was the many after-hours clubs around the city. One such club for gay people was Madame Peabody's Dancing Academy for Young Ladies in the basement of the Double Header (on the site of the Casino which opened in 1929). It was a special place like the Garden, but some didn't know it then. An after-hours gay dancing place was unheard of on the West Coast in the 1950s. What made it so unique was that men could actually dance with other men.

It was curious that when the payoffs stopped, Seattle became less wild. It was almost like the end of Prohibition. You had to be within the law after that. But the payoff system left a legacy in the gay and lesbian community. Though bars have their negative side, we were free to be ourselves and to discover each other in public. You just couldn't get enough of other gay people. It was a feast.

ROBY JACOME

Roby always has been a highly visible, uptown Seattle gay man. He was the Garden's maitre d' for many years. Semi-retired, he lives in Seattle's First Hill neighborhood.

★

I am a Seattle boy, born on September 28, 1920. My parents were good to me and I took care of my mother until she died at age eighty-seven. I came out when I was

★ Roby Jacome, who always dressed elegantly for his work as maitre d' at the Garden, works for the Ryding Co., a Seattle stationer.

eighteen but I never had any trauma about being gay. I never believed in being obvious about it so I never had any trouble. Drag is okay and I was never embarrassed to be on the street with Jackie Starr or Skippy LaRue, but Hotcha, no! Hotcha was too obvious. I never liked swishy queens or drags in public. I ran around with people who had class, what we used to call top-drawer, people who went to the Marine Room as opposed to the Double Header.

As maitre d' at the Garden I made $10 an evening. I was always hustling money to survive. The Garden was my second job. My daytime job was in the display department at Frederick & Nelson department store in the late 1940s for $17 a week.

I've always been into clothes. I've dressed well and always try to look like a million bucks. I looked my best when I worked at the Garden. I've still got the dress shoes I wore there—in perfect condition.

We had the seating area divided into several sections. The boys and the girls on the floor all wanted a fair share of the tips so I tried to keep them all filled in equal shares.

As people left, I'd move others up closer to the stage. I would also get tips for special seating.

People came from all over to the Garden of Allah. People came down there for kicks. It was like Finocchio's in San Francisco—a tourist trap. College kids thought it was "hip." Some were changed into a new way of living. People would think they'd see some promiscuity at the Garden, like gay people are always kissing and hugging each other. We hardly ever touched and the drags never came out and carried on between shows. They were professionals. We never had any trouble at the Garden. The only incident I can remember was when our off-hour policeman chased someone up the stairs for being rude.

Once a patron was caught smoking marijuana. That was serious and we had to appear before a judge but didn't have to go to court. The lawyer told me what to say and they worked it out because they didn't close us down. The Garden probably had to pay out some money. Of course, they had to pay off the police anyway.

Our show was local talent but some big names like Ray Bourbon performed there. He'd always dress in a skirt and a blouse, wear a sort of bun wig and sit on top of the piano and sing. We brought out the table cloths for that man, he was a famous act, he was tops.

Jackie Starr would come on and the place would become silent. Jackie had so much class that you were immediately under his spell. He had a beautiful body, not a blemish on him. On Sunday mornings, Frank Carlburg said he'd see Jack out of drag with a cigar in his mouth fishing off the pier below the Garden.

Then Hotcha would come on stage and destroy everything. She'd do anything for a buck. She was a carnival sideshow person, strong sell and naughty as hell. The audience would be spinning when she left the stage.

I got along well with the lesbians. They'd buy men's suits, keep the jackets for themselves and give me the pants. Some of the younger lesbians would have older sugar daddies.

Many people who played the Garden had carnival, vaudeville, burlesque, or variety experience. That's why everyone was so talented. They were real show business people. Frank Reid and Frank Carlburg who ran the Garden were real businessmen and kept the place going all those years. Carlburg's sister and her husband were partners with Frank. He wasn't around a lot and mostly took care of the books. I got along with Frank even though he had a dark side. He was a big drinker. He drank so much his mouth was round from beer bottles. He'd swirl the beer around the inside of his mouth before he swallowed it.

Duane Doan was Frank Reid's lover. He worked the bar and was a singing waiter. He'd sing Johnny Ray's "Cry" or another song called "The Little White Cloud That Cried" and tear off his tie and writhe in pain as the tears flowed from his eyes. We'd go over to Duane's house every weekend after the Garden closed with a bottle of whiskey. That was the way we unwound.

They made a lot of money at the Garden of Allah and they took every nickel home with them.

MOTHER CABRINI

Mother Cabrini was a native of the Seattle area, born July 18, 1926, in Newcastle, a mining community southeast of Seattle. He died in the summer of 1995. He described a difficult childhood with a mother who showed little affection and a father who beat him often. Once, angry because his mother had been slapped, he hurled a hot woodstove lid at the man he called Mr. Cabrini, cutting and scarring his face.

★

I finally couldn't take it anymore and left home at sixteen. I had a new job every three months. It was hard for me to stick to anything. I began to take bennies and in two months I was taking twenty-one a day. It got to be crazy. It was really hard to quit but I did. I had low self-esteem and I worried about being gay. It was years before I realized that there was nothing wrong with me—it was them. My life was a mess, or so I thought, but a miracle called the Garden of Allah came into my life.

I loved the Garden so much and used to go there every Friday and Saturday night for years. It was "our place," it was my place to find out who I was. All the people on the Orpheum and other theater circuits came down to the Garden. Mel Torme came down to the Garden from the Palomar Theatre. We called him "Melissa Hormone." He wasn't gay; we were just camping it up.

I've been playing around with drag since an early age. I don't know why, I just liked it. I'd put on my mother's high heels and dresses and play with my sister's dolls and paper cutouts. I never came out to my parents; I think my mother knew and Mr. Cabrini, but then he couldn't have hated me more anyway. I never was a performer; drag was fun time for me. Everyone called me Mother Cabrini.

I learned everything I know from Francine. We'd go to the Garden of Allah in drag. Francine was an outrageous, flaming queen who lived in Pioneer Square. She could turn a place upside down with her flamboyance and wit. She'd go up to the Mocombo filled with all the proper gays with ties and scream, "There are no men in here," and swish out the door. She'd buy a ten-cent bottle of perfume and pour the whole thing on her hair and she'd reek for days. She didn't like to shave her legs so she'd burn the hair off by the flame of her gas stove. It worked fine but it would sure stink.

It was hard to shop for clothes in the early 1950s. The proper stores like the Bon Marche and Frederick & Nelson would not have it. You could get by at Rhodes department store, but you couldn't push it. Drags went to the thrift stores a lot to buy women's clothes and wear them as is or made over. The Salvation Army thrift store at the Pike Place Market was my favorite store for women's clothes. I can remember in the 1940s there were still a lot of clothes left over from the '20s. I bought six flapper dresses there, but I eventually burned them with all my other drag clothes and pictures. I had wonderful beaded flappers. One was a full floor-length gown and weighed six and one-half pounds. That one created a sensation at the Garden one New Year's Eve.

I bought my falsies at the medical store at Eighth and Stewart. They had water or

★ Au Sing (Henry Chinn) was a member of the Luck Nigi Chinese Musical Club, a Seattle club that sponsored traditional Chinese theater and opera. Here, he played the traditional female role. In 1951, he rode on Ruby Chow's Restaurant float in Seattle's annual Seafair parade and was voted "the most beautiful Seafair princess." Chow, a former County Council member, commented, "We all knew he was a female impersonator but we didn't think anything about it."

something in them and they moved well. I also bought some falsies at Woolworth's for 98 cents, and I bought my bras and corsets there, too. Wigs were hard to come by, and they were expensive to rent at Brocklind's costume supply. Later I had a wig styled for me while I sat at Rhodes. Arman did the styling. It was terribly embarrassing; people stared and raised their eyebrows.

Au Sing was a beautiful Chinese boy and like a flower. An exotic dancer and stripper, he gave us a lot of tips about drag. Au Sing made me a pair of false eyelashes out of his own hair. He made eyelashes for everyone.

Mother Marge was an old drag queen who started going in drag around the turn of the century and continued to go in drag all her life. She was not an entertainer; she turned tricks, a hooker. Marge had a police record and I knew she shoplifted, but she was a sweetheart. I loved her. She had skin like a baby and was not even flabby. She'd

★ One shocked
audience of elderly
Chinese expected
Au Sing to perform
a traditional
Chinese dance, but
instead witnessed
a striptease with
fans to "Rhapsody
in Blue."

remove body hair with tweezers and Zip wax. She liked to cruise this men's room uptown. Once she got so angry at this other queen who'd sit in the next stall for hours and hours that she crumbled up some newspaper, lit it and threw it over the top of the stall on the queen, who fled.

Mother Marge cleaned the Double Header tavern for John and Margaret. She was in her seventies in 1955. Margaret loved Marge and helped her in her older years. She lived in a tiny hotel room nearby with the refrigerator in the bathroom. One day she was found dead in her room. Her closet was full of women's Goodwill clothes.

There was Gypsy, a carny; she'd sell anything for money or steal. Once we went into Florsheim's shoes and when we came out she asked me what I wanted from nine neckties and six pairs of socks she just stole from the store. I was shocked because I was with her all the time and I didn't see a thing. I always stayed away from her after that.

Mother Corrine was a black female impersonator in her seventies in 1950. She was poor and lived on a pension. I liked Corrine a lot, but not sexually as I had this thing about blacks then. You could always count on Mother Corrine to do a tap dance and splits at the Double Header. She was quite heavy and I don't know how she did it. She was always trying to kiss and hug me. I'd hug her but one evening she kissed me and I let her know that I was offended. Three days later she died and I cried and cried.[*]

Eventually, I gave up going in drag but still went to the Double Header after the Garden closed. I was with my lover Paul for fifteen years; he was killed in an auto accident. He was so sweet. My whole family adored him and mourned his death like one of their own.

Paul and I cared for my mother, who had polio, and Mr. Cabrini. After Paul died, I moved in with them and cared for them until they died. Mr. Cabrini went first. He told me on his deathbed, "You're a guardian angel but you're still a little bastard." Then mom died.

ISAAC MONROE

Isaac Monroe lives on Vashon Island in Puget Sound near Seattle. Monroe, who was born April 23, 1931, sells his paintings and plays piano with a group of musicians in local cafes. He represents those gays who disdained the Garden in its early years, for reasons he has only lately come to realize. Today, he sees it as a unique and wonderful place.

*

Before I had my first homosexual experience at age nineteen, I was like a lot of kids, trying to play the straight role but dreaming of men at night. A lot of gay people were coming out but it was still a dangerous move. Fear of exposure to family was serious but fear of police was terrifying, especially when you were just a kid from a middle-class family with no street smarts. Coming out often began on the streets. You were right out there in enemy territory and anything could happen. You could be terribly embarrassed, beaten up, and, the absolute worst, arrested!

One night on a double date we drove by Boldt's Cafeteria on our way to a high school dance and one of the boys looked out the window and said, "Queers go there." Boy did that go into my computer in a hurry. So one night I said to mother, "I'm going to a dance up at Queen Anne High School," and drove downtown to Boldt's.

[*]These comments should be understood in context of Seattle's wartime and postwar history. There were few African-Americans in Seattle before the war, and those who came to the city during the war generally did so to work in defense plants. Seattle had an informal line in the downtown section that separated clubs and bars frequented by blacks from those used by white residents. The Garden of Allah was north of the line, while jazz clubs and other after-hours places for blacks were located in what is now the International District to the south. The Garden crowds saw only a couple of black female impersonators and blacks, although not barred from the audience, did not visit the Garden in great numbers. Some of the Garden's musicians also played in black clubs, but no black musicians crossed the line enforced by segregated unions to work in the Garden.

I nearly lost my nerve, but I knew it was what I had to do. But when I went in and saw the people, I said to myself, "This is me?" All I saw were obvious queens with ducktail hair styles and their collars turned up blowing cigarette smoke ten feet in the air. Some used long cigarette holders, used them like they were dragon ladies, but it was the fashion then. But the queens used them for props. As they cruised people on the sidewalk through steamy windows, some of them smoked English Ovals—they were "sissy." Boys smoked Lucky Strikes.

I went down the cafeteria row and bought a cup of coffee. I sat down in one of those booths with the high backs and coat trees between each booth. Guys were sitting, kittering, and giggling around me, carrying on in the booths and staring at the sailors' baskets. I was hoping for something better. You feel it in the pit of your stomach, alone in a room of guys carrying on. To them, it was the usual gay scene, but for me it was extremely intimidating.

Ron, a good-looking twenty-four-year-old, was one of those young men. It took Ron no more than three minutes to get up from the table, walk over to my booth, sit down, and take over. "Hi. Never been here before?" He was very nice and patient, and helped me, pried me out. But those guys were good at prying people out—we were the potential tricks. I heard a couple of the guys say, "Blond Chicken," and "The golden boy has arrived."

Ron and I hit it off right away. I was so happy he was not like so many around me. He took me to one of those Japanese-run hotels nearby —nice, very clean—for $3.50 for two. It wasn't until he had me that night that he said, "You've never done this before." I said, "How could you tell?" He smiled and said, "Oh, I could just tell." It turned out he had found this person who didn't even know the word "gay."

The next week Ron said, "I'd like to have you over to my place to meet my mother." The next week I went to his place on Queen Anne Hill and this old queen came to the door with his teeth out. Ron said, "Isaac, I'd like you to meet my mother." I got hysterical and we all laughed. Then Ron said, "Now I'm going to take you down to the Garden of Allah."

I was not impressed. It was a rainy winter night. I remember the men on the street wearing long tweed coats with leather buttons—queens wore them like robes. Early vogueing. All I was seeing were these people—so much screaming. I was seeing the visible crowd; I was depressed. Where were the others? The all-American clean-cut boys like myself? Obviously, I was living a fantasy, but I didn't know it then.

We approached this dark, old building on First Avenue and Ron walked me up to the showbill with photographs of who's in the show. "Tonight, presenting Jackie Starr." His picture was there, very gorgeous. I just stared at his photograph. "She's not a woman," Ron said. I just didn't see it at all and at the time I was studying kabuki at the university. It was cold and rainy and now we had to go into the basement of this ugly, dank old place.

At the bottom of the stairs was the door into the Garden of Allah, and opposite it an old beat-up elevator. "What's up there," I said. "Oh, some of them live up there," Ron said. Guys who lived upstairs could pick up sailors at the Garden and take them up to their rooms. Behind a window with a round hole in the glass a voice screeched, "Yes?" Victoria, the ticketperson, was such an outrageous queen he made my head spin. Ron said, "He's a trick of mine. He's only nineteen; can you let us in?" "Well, I'm only nineteen myself," Queen Victoria snapped; "Come on in." He looked at me and said, "Honey, you're so cute, you're like a little lace doily."

If you saw Queen Victoria on the street during the day with eighteen people around you, he would just screech at you. He'd screech a half block away and come swishing up with his coat flaring and his collar turned up. He didn't care that he had broken your cover. He was saying, "You're going to come out of the closet and be yourself and you're going to stand up for what you are," but you were saying to yourself, "No, no, no."

My first impression of the Garden was of a blast of noise and smoke. The room was jammed. With its tile floor, it had the feeling of a New York City automat, but it was beautifully lit. They were so busy, I actually saw them dump the ashtrays right on the floor. Roby Jacome, the maitre d', held the door open for us and said, "Good evening, gentlemen." Roby was a cute gay guy who came out early, living the life, not just out of the closet as I was.

We came in when Kenny Bee and Francis Blair were on stage in camp drag, a routine called "The Two Old Bags from Tacoma." The place was in an absolute uproar and everyone was screaming with laughter. I looked at these two pathetic parodies of women and I was totally disgusted. It was all cock and sex jokes—looking up and reaching up each other's dresses—just dirty. But if I saw them today I would think they were hysterical.

The patrons and the tourists loved it—everyone was really into it. Bee and Blair had a bench in the middle of the stage where they sat down and started in on each other. They tore each other to pieces with insults. They deliberately did it all wrong—the costumes were wrong, the words were wrong, and the gestures were wrong for women and that just drove people crazy. "How can you act so queer," I thought.

But when Jackie Starr sang, I never got embarrassed. He sang all the songs I loved. His voice was soft, but strong, not falsetto, natural, a little bit of lilt, romantic. He stood very still as he sang his theme song, "As Time Goes By," with piano accompaniment. Jackie was brainy and polished. He wanted to be beautiful, for people to like him, to be chic. That night he was a Ginny Simms look-alike. His makeup was superb, not at all like a man trying to be a woman.

Another time he did an Arabian Nights dance routine accompanied by the pipe organ. He dressed in a sleek outfit and used finger cymbals going ching, ching, ching. When Jackie did this routine, he danced practically to the ground like those Middle Eastern dancers. He was so muscular that he could half squat coming across the floor and still do it gracefully. His dance was painfully long to me. It was probably only about seven minutes but I sat there and thought, "How long are you going to cruise around this room going ching, ching, ching?" Now I can see how professional he really was—his costumes, his body movements, that whole image. In a way it was so good it was beyond just illusion.

★ Jackie Starr's Arabian Nights dance was one of his most intense and muscular routines.

I lightened up when I saw Ray Bourbon. Ray was about forty years old when he came to the Garden of Allah. He was getting a little full in the middle and he seemed a husky sort of guy. When he came off with his bawdy lines, he had force. He was old enough to play a good Dame. He did a flawless Bette Davis. One evening as a Grand Madame he sang "I'll be seeing you" in a slow, deep, inebriated Tallulah Bankhead

★ The Garden's bartender got an appreciative laugh from impersonator Billy DeVoe.

voice: "I'll be seeing you in all the old familiar places.... In that small cafe, the park across the way—the park—it figures."

At the Garden he did a routine with a Duncan Phyfe table and a telephone. The phone would ring and he'd walk on and answer it. He would be on for about ten minutes, rattling on and on. His patter would come at you like bullets, bam, bam, bam. You're not through laughing at one thing when another one comes at you right in the face. No matter how crazy the audience got he would never wait for them to calm

★ Paris Delair, who appeared frequently in the Garden, began performing in his late teens, when he first experimented with drag in Vancouver, British Columbia.

down. He'd keep gittin' ya 'til he was through with ya. He'd rattle on about all the people he knew, gossipy stuff mixed in with outrageous jokes. After his show, he'd sit at our table. He would always try to seduce me like he was Rita Hayworth or somebody. I was extremely uncomfortable.

On weekends the Garden would be packed. Sometimes the bar would be three deep in sailors in civvies and uniforms. Above the bar a sign read "Off Limits." I did-n't go near the bar, I was afraid. One night they said, "Go over to the bar and stand there awhile. I stood there for a minute and two sailors and a soldier closed in on me. I was so speechless I scampered back to my table. I could not loosen up at the Gar-

★ Delair had one
of the most attrac-
tive bodies of any
of the Garden
dancers.

den. I should have made friends and even done something in the show. It would have added greatly to my stage experience. Ron used to say, "You can be so prudish."

One night several of us waited outside for some of the kids in the show to get dressed and meet us out front. After awhile Jackie Starr and some others came out. They were boys again. I thought, "Oh, now you're this way." Jackie walked all the way around me looking me over. I was shy and embarrassed. Jackie said, "I hear you have very good legs. You'd look good in a dress." I smiled at Jackie and tried to be as grateful as possi-

★ In his twenties, Delair was at his full potential as an exotic dancer.

ble, but I thought, "I'm trying to learn how to be a boy, I'm not trying to learn how to be a girl. I'm not Goldilocks, I'm Tom Sawyer. I've got enough problems as it is."

When Jackie looked me over, I knew damned well I was never going to do anything like that. But I did once and it was a total disaster. My lover and I went to this party and everyone was stunned to see me in drag and when they couldn't handle it, I lost

★ Paris Delair also toured the United States and Canada as well as appearing frequently in the cast of the Garden of Allah.

courage. My lover was so embarrassed and strangers asked me if he was my son. I guess I looked like someone's mother rather than someone chic like Jackie Starr. My lover avoided my company and I got drunk and made a fool out of myself and threw up in the kitchen sink. My lover drove me home as I puked out the window and groaned in agony on the floor in the back of the car. Let me tell you I was one ugly drag.

chapter 3

THE WOMEN: "IT'S OUR PLACE, TOO!"

★

In the Garden, lesbians enjoyed a bar that catered to them, even though they were generally outnumbered by the gay men in the audience. A woman could dance with another woman in many bars in the city, but the Garden fostered that intimacy. In that protective setting, Seattle lesbians went about finding partners and defining a public presence for the first time.

RITA KELSEY

Rita Kelsey's home north of Seattle still is a guesthouse for friends from the Garden of Allah. She owns the home she shares now with dogs and cats. She showed me scrapbooks crammed with pictures, including those of many of her friends from the Garden days.

★

I went to the Garden for the first time on April 2, 1947, with Nickey Arthur, my friend and lover. I'm not exactly gay myself and I'm not the other way. I don't know where I am although sex has never meant that much to me. My interest is where people are coming from. But I love gay people far more than the others.

There was a mix of lesbian and straight women at the Garden. Of course, there were lots of gay men and tourists and people who'd just drop in from the streets. To some, the Garden was beyond slumming and they wouldn't be caught dead there; others would come down just to see and snicker. They were disgusting.

One night two men and two women came down to the Garden all dressed up and very prissy. They sat at a table next to us. One of the women took an empty beer bottle with her when she went to the ladies room. I had to go, too, and this woman said to me, "You oughta have some protection coming in here. You know what kind of people are down here. They'd better not make a pass at me!" It was so funny really because one of the boys dressed as a girl was in there at the time.

Some of the lesbians would get into fights at the Garden; they'd get to drinking and arguing, but it wasn't bad. Not nearly as bad as Madame Peabody's. There have been some mean fights there, girls jealous of each other, half drunk, bottles flying. I always sat on the boys' side at Madame Peabody's. I didn't get along with the gay girls—the "Bitches" [butches]. They tried so hard to be men that they went way beyond what a man would be, in their language and everything. I didn't care for that.

There were not many masculine lesbians at the Garden, but there were many who tried to be. There were two different girls from Tacoma named Tony. The smaller one was fantastic. She wore a white tuxedo every time she came to the Garden. She had black hair and she was outstanding, but a heavy, heavy drinker. The other Tony I didn't care much for because she was a little on the rough side.

Most of the trouble was from straight people. They'd drink and make a remark and start something and Frank would throw them out. He tried to be neutral but the evenings were for the gay kids. Single men who came in off the street to get a beer sat at the bar in the back of the Garden. Straights would sit toward the rear near the bar, and the front was for the gay kids. We all had our own tables; if someone sat down before we got there, people at the next table would say, "That table is reserved." The regulars had it that way.

The Garden had a very homey feeling. The owners didn't allow any funny business. If any of the gay kids felt wild they went out the back door to the fire escape to carry on.

There were several Mickeys at the Garden, but Mickey Baasch was my friend and one of our crowd. Known as Nick Arthur, she was an emcee and sang every Friday and Saturday night for four years. She had a lovely tenor voice; she liked to sing the sad romantic songs like her favorite, "Maria Elena." She sang that song to me. Nickey's opening song was "If I Had My Life to Live Over." Nickey was adopted when she was just a few days old. She wanted to be a man so bad. We were together for twelve years, but she got so mean with her drinking that I couldn't take it anymore. I then took off with Bobby Kingville.

Bobby was a close friend and member of our crowd. Bobby and Nickey were both considered butches. Bobby was quite a dancer! She went in for the livelier numbers, especially the song, "Marie." She'd really get out there on the dance floor and carry on. If anybody tried to do something that Bobby thought was wrong, she'd go over like she was going to tear them apart, but they always wound up friends. Bobby wouldn't care if she got into a fight if it was necessary, but she wasn't the type to start a fight. She believed in fair play.

Gene Talbot was a soldier stationed at Fort Lawton who always came down to the Garden. He was a nice guy and he and Bobby hit it off. They liked each other and Gene shared his money with her. Eventually, they married. On their wedding night, Bobby and I got a room together and Gene spent the night with a police sergeant's son. I don't know why they got married, but Bobby got money and Gene had this idea of a respectable image for both of them. He wanted her to drop the butch image and dress up in a closet full of nice dresses. He'd run around with the boys but didn't want her to run around with the girls. He wanted her to play the part of a model wife and then he even wanted her to go around with their landlady, but Bobby was not interested. Bobby called me up and said, "I want to come home." They should never have married and just remained friends.

I married a straight man when I was a teenager, but it was a mistake. He was the serious type and I wanted to have fun, so we broke up. Many years later, I learned his wife had died so I sent Bill a sympathy card and enclosed my telephone number. He called me and we started going out and after three months, we got married, but this time it lasted seventeen years. I had to educate him about gay and lesbian life and he accepted it and grew fond of all my friends. He loved Bobby and tried to make friends with Nickey, but she was always so jealous of my other friendships. Bill tried so hard, but she was so mean to him.

I took care of Bill for nine months before he died. He had asbestos in his lungs. I got a call from his nurse at Bill's request to come to the hospital immediately. I said to the nurse, "How will I get there?" I don't know how Bill heard but he said, "Taxi!" And he said to the nurse, "Tell her I love her and I know she loves me." I got to the hospital and even though he couldn't see without his glasses, he saw me from across the room as I entered, then he took his last breath and died. He just wasn't going to go until I got there.

Nickey, Bobby, and I remained friends for over forty years, right to the end. Nickey went first in 1980. All she had was Social Security so her ashes were placed on a less expensive higher shelf at Washelli cemetery. Then Bobby got sick and I put her in the Crest House but it just wasn't her type of place. She was a veteran of World War II so I finally got her into the Veterans Home in Orting, Washington. She just loved it there and everyone treated her so well. She was there for about a year and a half before she died in 1984. I took care of the funeral arrangements for all three of them, the three loves in my life, Bill, Nickey, and Bobby. I had them cremated.

When Bobby died, I arranged for Bill's, Nickey's, and Bobby's ashes to be moved next to mine when that time comes. Four Garden of Allah pals resting beside each other for eternity. If it were still open, I'd still be going there.

Awhile back I wanted to walk by the building where the old Garden of Allah was and I saw that it had been torn down. I stood on that empty sidewalk dumbfounded. I wanted to cry. The Garden was fantastic, the greatest place on earth. There will never be another Garden of Allah, never.

GARDEN OF ALLAH

There'll never be another Garden
That can compare with you,
Or one with half your magic
Dear Garden we still love you.

The beautiful bonds of friendship
That we all once knew,

Many lasting for a lifetime
Garden of Allah we found in you.

You gave us joy and happiness
And calmed many of our fears,
You will be in our hearts and minds
Thru out all our years.

You are the one that's missed by many
Tho many years have passed,
Just one more night with you
Is all that we would ask.

    ★   RITA MILLER KELSEY, SEPTEMBER 1989

SHIRLEY MASER

Shirley Maser has been a visible butch in Seattle most of her adult
life. Born November 8, 1926, she has built a family, including her daughter and friends,
around long-term relationships. Maser drives cars from the Seattle-Tacoma Airport to
downtown locations for a car-rental company. She lives in a sparkling, comfortable
north Seattle home filled with antiques.

★

I loved the Garden of Allah. To me it was a home away from home. The first time
I went to the Garden I was just coming out. I was about twenty. Bobby and Big
Nick were the super butches at the Garden. I was in awe of Bobby and Big Nick.
I'd see Big Nick and Little Mick dressed up in tuxedos and I'd be in awe and think,
wow!—there's the gals dressed up like guys! I was pretty enthralled at the whole
thing.

At both the Garden and the Spinning Wheel the women and men sat apart. There
was no hostility. We all went down there for a purpose—to meet and be with people
of our own sex. I don't know of any incident where the men and women fought. We
all liked the Garden too much. No one wanted the bar closed because of trouble, so
we got along.

But Ann, who'd pull a knife, and Shirley and Max used to get into fights at the Garden. They were rough ladies. They'd throw Ann out periodically and Max once in
awhile. Another Mickey used to fight a lot; also her girlfriend Norma. Mickey was
married and had one hundred kids. God, she was tough! They fought a lot, they really
got into it, broken glass, tossed chairs, the whole bit.

In the 1940s when I was in my early twenties, I ran around with an all-female
motorcycle group. It was a national club called "The Motor Maids of America." I also
belonged to a local group called "The Queen City Motorcycle Club." There were
only about six in this club and I and the woman I was riding with were the only gay
women at the time.

★ Rita Kelsey was a good-humored catalyst for social activities involving Garden patrons.

Nationwide there were probably a lot more gays in motorcycle clubs but not the ones I rode with in the 1940s. We might have had the reputation of being gay—dykes on bikes—but it was more that we were "tough women," that type of woman. But we were cream puffs next to some of the bikers like the Hell's Angels. We went to motorcycle races and to hillclimbs and they had what was called "the mud run." I had a lot of fun in those days. There just wasn't that many girls riding motorcycles then. One of the reasons was getting branded for being a toughie or being gay, but it was also because of self-start. It took a lot of work to get them started. It would be like cranking up an old model T Ford. The gay girls didn't get into the motorcycle clubs here until the '50s. I'd be out riding with the straight girls but I could hardly wait to get down to the Garden where I could meet my gay friends, but I played it pretty straight.

★ Nick Arthur, who was an emcee and singer at the Garden, dressed to pass as a man. She was known for her widow's peak.

The Park Department sponsored sports events and I met a lot of women on these teams. The Park League then was "fast pitch." Now they have more "soft pitch" to give more women the opportunity to play the game. Back then almost all the women who played those ballgames were gay because they played a tougher ballgame because of the fast pitch. Many women can't play that caliber of game. Only the tough girls could do it and they were usually the butch gay women. Now it is more of a mix of straight and gay because of the slow pitch.

They also sponsored basketball. We also played against other towns such as Tacoma and Yakima. In basketball there was more inter-field activity. One field house would compete with another, but it was not a matter of one neighborhood against another. It was a lot of fun and it was also a way for women to meet other women. I can remember going to the Hub, which was Seattle's first lesbian bar, and seeing some of

★ Nick Arthur and Bobby Kingville were close friends and well-liked regulars at the Garden.

the girls on the team there and you knew damn well they were gay, but they would-
n't say S-H-I-T if they had a mouth full of it.

After the Hub closed, the Madison tavern was the lesbian bar, then the Grand
Union tavern opened up and a lot of older lesbians went there. That was in the 1950s,
and in the later '60s I opened the Crescent tavern on Olive Way and ran that for
years.

In the 1940s I can't remember any cruising places. In fact, back then every woman
thought she was the only lesbian in the world. Women then were often married.
They'd meet another gay woman in church and fall in love, or they were neighbors
or they met in the workplace. Two women I know were married for twenty years, met
each other, and divorced their husbands. As the gay bar scene developed that became
the main place to meet other women. Then there were lots of house parties, but most
of the people who went to those parties were already coupled. The parties were more
for recreation rather than meeting new potential lovers. When you went there you
knew who belonged to who; you didn't mess around with anybody. It was sort of like
straight people's parties or block parties.

I have had a charmed life. I had all the advantages—good upbringing, supportive
parents, a work ethic, and a sense of worth. I had my jobs and I just went ahead with

★ Shirley Maser rode in a women's motorcycle club, the Motor Maids of America, and visited the Garden regularly.

business, although I do feel there are times when one needs to speak up for the gay community. A lot of people have not had the advantages that I've had. Some people had things working against them. I've never had any problems because I've always been pretty open. If people can't accept that, then it's their problem. If I am labeled a "butch," that's okay because that's the way it is.

DR. PAT FREEMAN

"I have a Ph.D., you see, so I'm not viewed as lesbian but as eccentric." Pat Freeman called me after a brief report on my research was aired by a Seattle television station. She and Audrey Kalkstine, her partner of twenty-seven years, live in their home in the Wallingford neighborhood in Seattle. Freeman, whose graduate degree is in history, is a 737/747 program manager with the maintenance training department of the Boeing Co. Kalkstine, retired because of multiple sclerosis, volunteers with the MS Association of King County.

★

We, my twin brother Tony and I, were born on January 11, 1933, at Columbus Hospital in Seattle, later Cabrini Hospital. We were adopted at birth by Ann and Jack Freeman. Olive, a young college graduate, was hired to take care of us. Thus Olive became our nanny and she played a major role in our lives.

The Freeman home, however, was not by any means a stable home. Actually, dysfunctional might be an accurate description. Ann had a penchant for port wine and Jack was simply not too bright. I do not mean to suggest that we had a horrible childhood because we didn't. We had each other. And we had Olive who gave us love, security, and a strong sense of self. And Ann, for all her shortcomings, was a witty

★ Dr. Pat Freeman and her partner live in a friendly north Seattle neighborhood. As a teenager armed with false identification she watched the Garden's shows.

woman with a creative imagination. Both she and Olive gave us an appreciation of music, art, literature, and the theater. And Ann was employed, which meant that materially we were comfortable, at least by depression standards.

When we were thirteen, Ann died of a cerebral hemorrhage. Jack was not too interested in raising us, nor were we too interested in having him do so. Olive, however, did come to our rescue. And it could not have been easy for a single woman to raise two teenagers, and gay ones at that. Today Olive is ninety-two and we have come full cycle as I look after her welfare, but I do believe that homosexuality is not a subject that is part of her reality.

Tony and I recognized that we were gay by the time we entered Lincoln High School in 1947. Unfortunately, this was a time of oppression and social conformity. Witch hunts for commie pinkos and homos were making headlines. There was no open gay society. Everyone was in the closet. Gays and lesbians were viewed as perverted and the lowest of the low. And the laws reflected this. The gay bar scene was often furtive and, for some, guilt-ridden.

Frankly, guilt was not something I had about being a lesbian. But sadly, my brother did. He could not cope with society's view of gay life. He had problems with it to the degree that it eventually affected our relationship. I think he would have preferred that I had been straight, gotten married, had children, and led this idealized life—that he would have lived vicariously. I doubt that he ever really accepted being gay and he certainly never accepted my lesbianism. As a result, we basically went our separate ways.

It was in high school that the Garden of Allah became my introduction into the gay scene, but Tony would never go. He saw it as seedy and disreputable. It would have been nice to have shared the gay aspect of our lives. That will remain a major regret in my life.

There were probably six to ten gay students that we knew about outside of my immediate high school group, plus a number that were the subjects of speculation. And then, of course, there was the faculty.

I was seventeen when, with my best friends, Rex and Bob, I first went to the Garden. Rex impersonated Hildegard at an assembly in 1949 and none of the students recognized him. When we were seventeen Rex got to know Thelma, the [police] matron at the Garden, and talked Bob and me into going down there. This was, of course, the absolute ultimate in growing up, to go into a tavern and not get kicked out and then to be with our own kind. This was butterfly time. To this day I do not know why she let us in, and continued to do so. I think she just took pity on us.

Our pact was that we'd go together and leave together and we would only have soft drinks. Our goal was to get in the door without being tossed out. The next step was getting to a table without any questions from the waiter.

The first time was, of course, a bit scary. We were under age and this was THE gay cabaret. And we did indeed hold to this the entire time of our association with the Garden. We would arrive early, before the door charge and cabaret prices went into effect. Mostly we drank Coke or occasionally Rex or Bob would have a beer. We were rather conservative about the whole thing and spent quite a bit of time looking out for the liquor inspectors, who always wore dress hats with the brim pulled down. It was a poor man's FBI look.

I believe we were the only teenagers that regularly went there. At least, I do not recall seeing any others. There were no support groups for gay teenagers, let alone for gay adults. The Garden was our entree into the gay world; it was our support group. We met gay people; we got to know Jackie Starr, Francis Blair, and other performers. We went to their parties, we were accepted, and they became our family. It was our refuge from society's homophobia and we could be ourselves. Besides the entertainers were tops.

I remember the first Halloween party that Rex and I attended at the Garden. This was a big event for us and we went in style. We went to Brocklind's and he rented a gown and heels and I rented a top hat, white tie, and tails. They were a bit uptight about this at Brocklind's. On the big night we took a cab to the Garden. Rex did quite well in heels from the house to the cab, but heels on cement sidewalks is a lot different from heels on carpet. He suffered a bit from bent ankles. Bob as a sailor, Rex as the gowned beauty, and me as the Tareyton man swept into the Garden. And while one would like to think that all heads turned in admiration, I am afraid that the cabby's head turned in utter dismay.

For awhile I spent a lot of time with the gay men because of my friendship with Rex and Bob. There was not the animosity then between the men and the women. We were all in the same boat and we had a camaraderie born of oppression, if nothing else. I began to meet a lot of lesbians but they were very leery of me because I was "jail bait" and a walking twenty-year sentence. It was tough on me. Eventually I was accepted and invited to parties. I am still friends with a number of those women.

I recall giving a bad time to the straight women tourists who came to see the show and watch the queers. They would go to the ladies room in pairs, for protection, I suppose. I stood around and stared at them and generally made them uncomfortable. It was rather juvenile, but fun.

There was a big butch called Big Bobbie, a tough old dyke. She always wore men's suits. She left the Garden one evening and went to a tavern in Pioneer Square. She took exception to a straight male there and proceeded to knock his head against a wall. It was an absolute must then for the gay crowd to go to that tavern to see the hole in the wall.

I distinctly remember that the lesbian community was into role-playing. Those were the days of butch and femme. At best it was repressive and in the long run, I believe, all that sexual rigidity created problems. Those butches were "touch me not." Their role was to make love to the femme and generally be the man of the house.

A butch could not, dare not, admit to wanting or having her femme reciprocate when making love. If it ever became known that this actually happened then the butch was said to have "rolled over," and this was the ultimate disgrace. Oh yes, the femme had restrictions, too. She was to be passive—never too aggressive. It was all very heterosexually based. All the sexual restrictions of the straight society were picked up and adapted by the lesbian community. And this led to added oppression and confusion, as well as a certain amount of sexual frustration.

Women then were not promiscuous like the men; there was no opportunity and they did not hang out in parks or restrooms. A lot of the women were coupled, but a certain number were unattached. Those women would cruise a couple and maybe even break them up. A number of women had this reputation, and I think these people are now essentially alone in life. The promiscuity of these women would be actively exchanging partners.

As a teenager, my reaction was that role-playing was absolutely strange. I must have been one of the new breed. I can still remember the shock and disbelief that ran through the lesbian scene when a butch left her femme and took up with a butch, God forbid, as a femme. Unfortunately, the sexism of the period was emulated, too.

It seems sad that it was the straight society that was emulated instead of the lesbian culture of the 1920s and '30s with lesbians such as Djuna Barnes, Romaine Brooks, Natalie Barney, and Sylvia Beach as role models. These women were all gradations of masculine and feminine and were proud of their lesbianism.

In the 1960s, younger women who were experimenting with gay and straight sex broke down the rigidity and role-playing. I think the sexual philosophy of today would make Barney and Brooks smile.

chapter 4

AMATEUR NIGHT

★

Wednesday was amateur night at the Garden of Allah. Prizes were free drinks or a week's booking on the show. Emcees worked hard to find performers, and often recruited patrons ahead of time to volunteer. Hal Hanson, who lives in Tacoma as he did when he visited the Garden regularly, said you could expect anything on amateur night. "It was just anybody who could do something whether they were good or not, people who'd go on just for fun. They had magicians, dancers, singers, everything." Others told of jugglers and performing dogs.

I interviewed three men who performed in amateur night shows. Jim Gerlach, who was born May 24, 1926, died in 1991. Melcohm McCay still resides in Bremerton, a city across Puget Sound from Seattle. Born October 30, 1930, Countess Estelle was a cook for many years at the Thirteen Coins and other popular Seattle restaurants. Doing drag solely as a hobby, he performed in hundreds of shows in Pacific Northwest cabarets, at USO shows, and at private parties. He died in the summer of 1995.

JIM GERLACH
★

I first went to the Garden of Allah when I was twenty years old. I didn't see the Garden as all that attractive, but I knew right away that it was my place. I was not shocked by the gay life and drag scene because in San Francisco a merchant seaman picked me up and took me to a gay party and to Finocchio's.

I was going to the University of Washington and would get out of school around five p.m. Friday. Then we'd go down to the Garden when it opened around six. They didn't charge admission—about a dollar—until eight. Pitchers of beer would be 75 cents. My crowd always sat at two tables put together in front of the stage. My best friend, Billy, and I dyed our hair platinum and we were pretty flamboyant. We'd camp outrageously.

Jackie Starr was the first drag I met at the Garden. We became lifelong friends. Jackie would say, "There are a lot of people who'd like to know you. They want to sit with you and buy you drinks. You're kinda cute but so crazy. If it isn't a truck driver or a serviceman, you won't even look at them." Billy and I used to get into Jackie's makeup and just lay it on thick. Jackie'd say, "You wear as much makeup just walking down the street as I wear in a week." Now, when I see drags wearing too much makeup I want to hit them with a stick.

On amateur night, Jackie would drag Billy and me back to the dressing room and dress us up. We were so bad we were good. We often won because sometimes there would be no one to go in the show. For a prize, we'd get maybe $10 or some pitchers of beer. Everyone knew us so they'd go overboard with the screams and applause.

Later, I teamed up with Pete and did some shows at an Oakland bar. On opening night in Oakland we did a wild routine called "Love for Sale." I had this short dress with a slit up one side and Cuban heels with my feet sticking out both ends. I didn't shave my legs and I wore no stockings. Somewhere I got a Dolly Parton brassiere—I had tits out to here. Our wigs weren't even combed. Our first show was a success; the audience screamed with laughter. After our show the owner came up to our dressing room and she was angry. "For God's sake," she said, "are you trying to close my place?" I had Jockey shorts on, but every time I'd do a high kick, the audience got a generous display of private parts. For the next show, my lover's mother went into the ladies room and took off her bloomers and gave them to me.

At the Garden we'd drink a little beer before we'd go out and make fools of ourselves. We had to drink to get up nerve to go on stage, but once we got out there, anything went.

What did surprise me about the Garden was the number of lesbians. It was their place, too. That suited me fine because I have always felt that gay men and lesbians should stick together. Nickey and Bobby, two outstanding lesbians, both wore double breasted suits. Nickey was emcee and a very good singer. She went with Little Rita, who wore Mary Pickford curls. Rita was kind of conservative. She worked for the government and absolutely hated cussing.

Sometimes the lesbians got into awful fights on the dance floor, especially if one looked at another gal. It was okay to look at a guy because a few of the lesbians would sleep with them for the money. But most of the men and women behaved themselves. It was mostly the butches who got rough.

Prostitutes came down to the Garden from Bellingham, about eighty miles north of Seattle. They just loved the gay kids. They'd sit at our tables and we'd exchange hot stories and just have a ball. I never knew straight men could be so kinky. They'd tell us wild stories about all the city fathers, but never mention any names.

Once the prostitutes came down to the Garden with two Army officers and made them take us to lunch at the Olympic Hotel. We were in drag and they were drunk enough not to notice. They tried their damndest to screw us but we told them we were nice girls and were saving ourselves for marriage. I didn't tell them that I was already married.

Doris, a lesbian friend, wanted to get out of the Army, so we got married. Doris and the Army gal were both in love with Nickey, the emcee at the Garden. Nickey was best man and the other Army gal was matron of honor. After we were married, Doris and the matron of honor got into this passionate embrace and Nickey and I stood with our arms around each other. The poor justice of the peace was just dumbfounded. He just stood there speechless. Doris moved to Australia and I never saw her again. We were never divorced.

Lots of servicemen went to the Garden but around 1948 a gay serviceman turned in another one for being gay to get even (they had been lovers.) The military sent spies to the Garden to collect names. The spies tried to engage us in conversation to get our names and match them with statements by suspected military homosexuals. They were so obvious it was funny. They were so petrified at being in such an evil, disgusting place that they'd almost shake. We'd tease them by walking past them or sitting next to them at the bar and acting very nelly. They'd give us these awful looks like we were really sick, but they didn't find out a thing.

I ran with an older crowd. Two older men loved to be with younger men, so each had an entourage when they'd go out. They'd try to outdo each other and when the two groups would meet at the Garden, they'd sit and glare at each other.

It was special when one of the performers sat at a table between shows. It was called a "courtesy call." When Jackie sat at your table, that was a special honor. Jackie had such charisma.

Between shows the organist would play the pipe organ for dancing. The girls could dance with each other, but heaven forbid if the boys did. But we devised a way. We'd line up in a chorus line with arms locked and ask the organist to play, "I'm looking over a four-leaf clover." We'd be out there kicking our legs up and have a good time. I'm sure the tourists got a big kick out of us.*

A wonderful old drag queen named Jeannie Evol was close to seventy when she played the Garden. You couldn't help thinking of her as a funny little man in drag but so funny. You'd just look at her veins and crack up. One of her routines was "Glow Worm." She'd sing and dance draped in a long string of battery-powered lights. It was absolutely so ridiculous, but wonderful. Once she got arrested in the men's room at the Pike Place Market. Her agent was angry with her, but Jeannie said, "Well, if you would find me a trick once in a while I wouldn't have to sit in public toilets." The last

---

*Seattle gays and lesbians apparently were persuaded by their police "protectors" that there was an ordinance forbidding same-sex dancing. In due time, someone discovered that the only law was one that required a cabaret license if there was any dancing at all.

★ Jim Gerlach performed for amateur night prizes, a few dollars or pitchers of beer. Photo, left, was taken about 1948; the one on the right in 1991, shortly before his death.

time I saw Jean Evol was at Finocchio's in San Francisco. She was one of the "Old Bags from Oakland." Poor Jeannie never made it to the finale because she was passed out on the dressing-room floor.

Performers from the Garden would always be invited to gay parties in those days. When they came in drag, it was special. One night Jackie went to one of those parties but left her apartment key in the dressing room at the Garden. Her landlady at the Governor Hotel, a Japanese-American woman, refused to believe this woman at her door was the same Jack Starr she knew. Jackie finally had to take off her wig to convince her.

I feel I've had a good life. When I was in Rome on a tour of the Vatican, after everyone had left the gallery, I reached up and touched the big toe of Michelangelo's "David." I always thought of David as the perfect male. If nothing else had happened to me, at least I can say I touched the big toe of David.

MELCOHM MCCAY

★

      I first went to the Garden in 1947. It had a warm atmosphere and a hot reputation. There was a certain stigma attached to the Garden. You could be crit-

★ This photo shows Jackie Starr dressed for the street in 1947. While police often harassed men in drag, Starr easily passed as a woman on Seattle streets.

icized for being a female impersonator or someone who hung around that scene. One wanted to be accepted and not stereotyped in those days. It was difficult to feel good about ourselves; we only heard the negatives about being gay.

They were always trying to get people to go on amateur night on Wednesdays.

To Jackie & Bill. Hope I have the pleasure of working with you again. Your og great Kate S[...]

★ A regular Garden artist, rather than an amateur, Jan Janssen sang popular songs in the style of Kate Smith.

They managed to talk me into it a few times, especially after a few drinks. So, I'd drop my somewhat puritanical self and go in the show. I did it for drinks because I had no talent and I wouldn't get a booking.

One night Phil Meager and another lesbian friend taught me a song that I could sing on amateur night, "My Queer Racketeer."

★ Countess Estelle
was an amateur-
night hit, and later
played in USO shows
and straight clubs,
always as a female
impersonator.
Updating the tradi-
tional vaudeville
Prima Donna, he
performed more
in the style of
contemporary
pop singers.

I wish you were here
My queer racketeer.
That big boy so sweet, and oh gee,
When I play with his gun,
Do I have fun!
I handle it so tenderly.

I almost spoke the words because I couldn't sing, but I did look rather well in drag. It was like an old Mae West song, kind of stupid and not very memorable, but I won free drinks that night.

Another amateur night Jim Gerlach and I did an improvisational act together. Jackie Starr loaned us some outfits and wigs. Part of our routine was a mock fight; we'd take our wigs off and hit each other with them. Jackie was not pleased to see the props abused, but he was very decent about it, and we learned a lesson.

I will never forget the night I got arrested at the Garden of Allah. In 1947, I was going to art school in the evenings and on the way home I'd stop and have a drink at the Garden, which was on my bus route. I sat with friends and there was this cute little sailor with us. On a whim he gave me a little kiss. That caused an awful commotion. Mom, the police matron, saw us and strong-armed us up to the street and told the police there "to take these two queers to jail." I didn't think there was a law against it; one ought to be able to kiss a pig if he wants to. The sailor asked what the charge was and they knocked him down, roughed him up, and threw him into the drunk tank. We spent the night in jail and were released the next morning after we paid a fine. It was a very traumatic experience. After we got out of jail, we checked into a motel and had mad passionate sex. We parted and never saw each other again. Ships that pass in the night.

COUNTESS ESTELLE
★

I was ten years old when I'd put on that brown stocking makeup and get into a grass skirt and play Betty Grable. I'd walk around the neighborhood and I thought I was a big star. But the kids would point at me because I was fat.

In high school I sang with a western band. We did school shows as well as USO shows all through 1946 and 1947. The director of the USO show suggested I go in drag and be billed as a novelty act. It worked so great that I began doing my act at school shows. The kids accepted me. If they asked me if I was gay I'd say, "Oh, no." I hardly knew what gay was.

I knew about the Garden of Allah when I was in high school because my mother and her friends used to stop in there for a drink after work at Swedish Hospital. Earl Steves played the drums there and also drove the No. 2 Madrona bus they rode on. I remember riding on the same bus with soldiers stationed at Fort Lawton who'd be talking about going to the Garden of Allah for a blow job.★

In 1947, each person in our literature class was supposed to write to a prospective employer. I wrote to Frank Reid, one of the Garden's owners, asking him for a part in the show at the Garden. I was so nervous when I went down to be interviewed.

★Many people believed that sex was commonplace at the Garden, but that was wishful thinking. No club owner would have permitted sexual activity. It would have been suicidal.

I've interviewed for Tex Ritter, the Andrews Sisters, etc., and I was always nervous, and even shook, but once I was on, it was okay. I guess my fear was that they wouldn't like me. Frank Reid liked me and invited me to be on amateur night, but since I was underage I had to stay in the dressing room and have a chaperone. My mother was the chaperone that night, but she said, "I can't do this every night." But that was okay, drag was a hobby to me. I always approached it as a professional would, but I never wanted to make a living at it. Later, my mother made sweaters for all the kids in the show and they'd come over to our house and party.

I was at ease with the tourists in the Garden. I feel more popular with them than with gay people. I've done hundreds of straight shows, such as American Legion, the Elks, Eagles, Civil Air Patrol, and Police Reserve from Tacoma to Bellingham. I always tried to get along with everybody, but I especially tried to get along with the musicians. If something goes wrong, I don't blame them as many do.

Flossie and Flo were barmaids at the Garden and Flossie was also a police matron at one time. Her daughter was around the Garden a lot and then she married a policeman and he was around a lot.

Jan Janssen sang in the show and had a terrific Kate Smith voice and stage presence. She was a very large woman and when we danced we were a "ton of dancers." I have been up and down the weight scale. Once I weighed four hundred pounds; now I've slimmed down.

A lot of the strippers and girls on the line at the Rivoli liked the Garden and the female impersonators, and some worked there. June Morgan did a routine called "The Beauty and the Beast," half-woman, half-man. She'd lay on a sofa and caress herself and the illusion was great. Evon and Nicoli were dancers at the Garden and the Rivoli. Nicoli was black and Evon was white and very exotic and dynamic. Evon was also a good stripper.

Straight women like drags and lesbians like drags, but most women think that drags don't act like women, more like silly little girls. Many drags are too flashy. They try to shock people for attention. But Francis Blair told me, "Real female impersonators don't act like that."

When we went out we used to start at the Market and drink all the way down First Avenue to Pioneer Square. The Garden was definitely a watering hole. I'd often be in drag and the police didn't like that. Drags rarely went out on the streets in the 1940s, '50s, and '60s. The police would hassle you all the time, especially if you were prostituting. Some were.

I didn't really have a bad time with the police, some cat and mouse things, but nothing serious. I knew a lot of them and they knew me. They'd holler at me and I'd holler back. I didn't think it was so bad that they had to holler at me. They didn't want me to go in drag on the street or drive my car to the parking lot behind the Double Header and walk to it in drag, and they didn't want me to be in drag in Pioneer Square when I wasn't working. A lot of that came from McCarthyism.

I've always wanted to have a sex change. Since I was five, I've felt more like a woman than like a man. I feel more at home in straight society. I always thought I'd be a better person as a woman instead of having to do all this gay stuff. I never picked up men or cruised in restrooms; I've never had a satisfactory sex life; I didn't want to mess up my makeup and costumes!

I feel Countess Estelle is the real me.

chapter 5

THE JEWEL BOX REVUE

★

During the 1920s, a flood of Prima Donna female impersonators came onto the speakeasy, theater, and burlesque scene. The art of impersonation, elegantly revived at the turn of the century by Julian Eltinge, a top attraction on the vaudeville circuit, went into decline until the late 1930s. In 1939, Doc Benner and Danny Brown, lovers and fellow New Yorkers, produced the first *Jewel Box Revue*. They declared in their programs, one of which I have in my collection, that they had set out to "bring back the glories of a neglected field of entertainment, to bring back female impersonation as a true art." Sophisticated in the arts, they were able to discern popular taste and from their carnival experience knew how to promote it.

Benner and Brown skyrocketed to the top in the nightclub field. They combed the country for the finest talent and staged some of the most lavish and spectacular song-and-dance reviews ever seen in show-wise metropolitan cities. "We hope to reach in the nightclub field what the great Julian Eltinge reached in the theater—artistry and showmanship combining for a thrilling evening's entertainment," they declared in their programs.

The *Jewel Box Revue* traveled all over the country and Canada and in 1946 opened the Garden of Allah to a "smashing success." Doc, who was several years older than Danny, sang and performed in the *Jewel Box* and handsome, muscular Danny was the master of ceremonies.

Jimmy Kelly, a Seattle man who was a regular patron of the Garden, told me that Danny was the "darling of women," like the New York madam who set Doc and Danny up in the Jewel Box Club in Miami. They took the show on the road in the summer and operated out of the club in the winter. In Minneapolis, a beautiful prostitute gave Danny everything and when they opened the Garden all the madams in town came to see the show and absolutely fawned over Danny, Kelly said.

Jerry Ross, an impersonator in the show, said the *Revue* had a strong comic flair. "You were making fun of yourself, so to speak, so society could accept you. If you were serious, the public would be

★ One of the most popular acts on cabaret bills for a decade, *Bee Vester's Beef Trust Revue*, five hefty women singers, played the Garden. The group, whose slogan was "A thousand pounds of mirth and girth," was the postwar reincarnation of an 1890s act, "Billy Watson's Beef Trust Beauties."

offended so you kept it light, a novelty." He said that while gays came to see the show, it was not geared for them. It was the straight audiences that supported the *Revue*.

The *Jewel Box Revue* could be viewed as an early gay organization—gays, lesbians, bisexuals, and transgenders in financial, artistic, and social partnership. In thousands of performances over twenty-five years, the *Revue* kept the early gay community focused on who they were.

The *Revue* always featured a comic and in its last four-week engagement at the Showbox in Seattle, Art West was the house comedian. Ross said that West was very funny, and talked like an exaggerated society matron with a deep, caustic tone. Everybody was an "evil queen" or a "nasty queen" to West. He had trunks filled with old pictures of burlesque and vaudeville people. Ross said West "was from the old school of female impersonators—never get into the sun, beautiful white skin, powder everything down, very gay nineties, accentuated makeup, very much a lady, proper, but he could still have fun." He had been a vaudeville success in the team of Durand, West, and Durand—Three American Beauties. They were female impersonators about 1920.

Art West, like most impersonators, was not one to take a homophobic insult. Some-

★ The *Jewel Box Revue* cast in 1939, its first year, included, from left, Pepper Cortez, Danny Brown, Jackie Starr, Doc Benner, Gita Gilmore, and Polish Princess.

one made a rude remark to him as he entered the Showbox Theatre. Art snapped back and the guy hit him, knocking him to the sidewalk where he hit his head and died. The newspapers, showing their reluctance to acknowledge gays, scarcely mentioned the incident.

Seattle singer and actor Ben Shepherd replaced Art West and "got rave reviews from everyone who saw the show." Shepherd remembers, "This was when the show advertised '20 Men and One Woman.' The woman, Storme De LaViere, who had a deep baritone voice, was the only member of the cast billed as a male impersonator and the rest of us might dress either as men or women, depending on the routine. One night the narcotics squad came by on a search for drugs and the costume maker, Miss Corday, frantically sewed all his bennies into the piping of his hat. He was just putting on the hat when the narcotics men came through the door."

Jerry Ross worked in clubs on his own and in carnivals as well as in the *Revue*. What follows is his story.

JERRY ROSS
★

I joined the *Jewel Box Revue* in Fort Worth, Texas, right after the Second World War. The *Jewel Box* and the *Beef Trust Revue* were the two best-grossing

★ Gita Gilmore, a sensational comedian, was an original member of the *Jewel Box Revue* and played the Dame at the Garden in the 1940s.

shows on the night club scene. The *Beef Trust* was five very heavy women singers. They were so funny and they had such pretty faces.

The *Jewel Box Revue* had a huge truck that not only carried everyone's luggage but also carried ten or twelve production numbers. It was a tremendous amount of costumes and sets and trunks. They needed all the different production numbers because

★ By the time the *Jewel Box* was the opener at the Garden of Allah in 1946, the cast was bigger and the show was much more polished. Doc Benner is second from left, Danny Brown is in the center of the back row, and Paris Delair is second from the right; the others are not identified.

sometimes we'd stay a long time in one place and as business dropped off we'd change production numbers. That would bring in new business. There were a couple kids in the show that had a car so I'd usually ride with them. A couple of times I took the train. Doc and Danny would give the drivers a little extra money for gas. We didn't always stay in nice hotels; sometimes we stayed in real dumps. One place didn't even have a lock on the door. The desk clerk said, "Take it or leave it; I'll just rent it to someone else."

While I was with the show we never had any trouble with the police. Doc and Danny ran a good ship. It was business and you didn't cause any problems.

The *Jewel Box Revue* was a flash-act show, one filled with glitter and upbeat music and backed by a line of singers and dancers. They always did three big production numbers. The middle number was usually a black light number, like "Slaughter on 10th Avenue." The chorus girls' and boys' hands would glow and they did a lot of hand work, and the adagio team, a duo who performed ballet-style lifts, turns, and spins, was worked into the scene and then the dramatic slaughter scene.

One production number they used to do was "Artists and Models" and they would dance to "Paravan," a semiclassical composition. The boys dressed as girls wore longer tutus with net skirting and the fellows who weren't in drag wore silver lame artist

★ Precious poses were the trademarks of the *Jewel Box* cast. Paris Delair is at far right.

smocks and berets and held painters' pallets and brushes. Most of the production numbers had a little comedy thrown in.

Jerry Sherman, Danny's brother-in-law, was the musical director and he did all the arrangements. Almost all the clubs then had a house orchestra. This was a time when night clubs were very popular in America—before television. The orchestra would rehearse the music and the kids would come in and do a walk-through rehearsal.

Both Doc's and Danny's mothers traveled with the show. Danny's was a typical Jewish mama. She took care of her little boy. She was very stern but she was also a very loving person. Once in Florida she was ill in the hospital. She had never missed an opening night so she hired an ambulance to take her to the show. She wasn't going to miss her "faggilist," as she affectionately called him.

I worked under the name of Jerry Ray in the *Revue*. I sang solo and danced in the numbers. Two of my songs were, "Tonight You're Going to Sleep in the Bathroom, Papa," and "The Spinach Song." "The Spinach Song" went:

> I didn't like it the first time,
> but I was so young you see.
> But I've smartened up and I've gotten wise;
> now I've got enough for two dozen guys.
> I didn't like it the first time,
> but oh how it grew on me."

★ "Two bucks ain't enough for Shanghai Flo," Jackie Starr was saying in this *Jewel Box* pose from the late 1930s.

The *Revue* made money but we never saw much of it. I was promised $75 a week but they said business was bad so I only got $50. It wasn't quite enough after you paid your hotel, etc. When I joined the show, the star was Jackie Maye. He probably got around $200 a week. He deserved the pay because he was so talented and popular. He was a supreme Prima Donna and singer, like Jackie Starr.

★ By the 1950s, the *Jewel Box* staging was much more lavish. Paris Delair, left, joined three unidentified beauties for an Arabian Nights routine.

I liked Doc and Danny, but I felt they cheated everybody; I got along better with them when I wasn't working for them.

One of our featured stars was Laverne Cummings, who I believe is still at Finocchio's. He had his own long hair and they built a production number around him. He modeled himself after Arlene Dahl. He did his production number to the song, "I Love You So Much."

We always had a ballerina on the show. When I was on the show, our ballerina was Kenny Renard. He was billed as "Our male toe dancer, a ballerina supreme. She'll tiptoe into your hearts, dance on your table and tiptoe into your glasses." Kenny was near-sighted and once at Sofie's Cat and the Fiddle Club in Cincinnati, Kenny danced right on the tables. There were no footlights on the stage and the tables were on the same level as the stage. I don't know how she did it; she'd make a turn and be on a table and not even realize it.

Leon LaVerde was a successful dancer, but up in his years. He tried to do an arabesque with the other kids; they stand with one foot flat on the floor and the other leg extended straight back. But Leon's other foot never left the floor.

When Cleo, who was raised in an ethnic neighborhood of Detroit, was a kid, a neighbor woman complained to his mother about the prostitute out in front of the saloon—green dress, red shoes, purple blouse, etc. "That's no prostitute," his mother said, "that's my son."

We stayed a long time in the cities on the circuit, and often we'd go back and play the city again and again. We always played the Apollo in New York. It had a large black cast at that time. There would always be writeups in the newspapers. In Denver, someone filmed the whole show. If it still exists, they have some rare footage.

We went into the Turf Club in Denver with a two-week option and stayed eighteen weeks. We were in the newspaper and did TV interviews and got terrific business. Another club, the Tropics, featured a stripper called Native Dancer. And Native Dancer was one of the most popular horses running. It was the leading money-winning horse in 1953. The club put a big ad in the local papers saying, "The Tropics features all girls—real girls—and Native Dancer." It was a homophobic response to the *Jewel Box Revue* or maybe just a cheap shot to get more business. Doc and Danny put an ad in the papers which said, "The all-boy plus one girl revue at the Turf Club extends their best wishes to Native Dancer in her run for the roses."

chapter 6

BACKSTAGE WITH THE CAST

★

Shows at the Garden of Allah came alive for me as I interviewed the singers, emcees, impersonators, and other cast members.

WANDA BROWN

Wanda Brown was the master of ceremonies at the Garden for years, and she sang solos in some of the shows. She had been singing in jazz clubs for years when she arrived in Seattle in 1943. Her picture is in a permanent display about Seattle's jazz history at the Seattle-Tacoma International Airport and she was featured in *Jackson Street After Hours*, a 1993 history of Seattle's jazz scene. She was married to the late Vernon Brown, a well-known Seattle jazz drummer. She still sang at Patti Summers' club until shortly before her death in 1995.

★

I was born on July 7, 1919, in Oklahoma City. I've had no formal training as a musician, but my father was a fiddle player. My brother was a great bass player and my mother, who played the piano, had a band that included Jack Teagarden. I grew up with music. I learned how to read music and was always going to different clubs and trying to sing. I got into singing around the key. I sound a little like Billie Holliday, but my favorite was Ella Fitzgerald.

When I was twelve years old, I walked into one place in Oklahoma City and told them I'd like to be in the show. They hired me right away. I stood up there in the wings and posed with the rest of those gals with the scanty clothes on. But I didn't do any stripping or anything, it was just a background pose. Then sometimes I'd stand at the side or sing while the stripper was on. You wouldn't be able to get away with something like that now, being twelve years old, but they didn't have the laws they have now. If you were big enough, you were old enough.

At the Garden, I tried to do more of the peppy songs, such as "All of Me," "Sunny Side of the Street," "Pennies from Heaven," "Ballin' the Jack," "Foggy Day," and "Let Me Off Uptown." Ballads were easier for me to sing because I'm basically a torch singer. I liked "Fools Rush In," "More Than You Know," "Solitude," "Trust in Me," "Body and Soul," "I Cried for You," "Don't Blame Me," "Good for Nothing Joe," "I've Got It Bad and That Ain't Good," "The Man I Love," and "You Came to Me from Out of Nowhere."

I also did some suggestive material, not real naughty, just enough. Songs like "King Solomon—It Takes a Good Man to Do That." It goes, "Now he had sweethearts by the score, but then married seven hundred, I don't know, maybe more. It takes a good man to do that, etc." "Elevator Man" was pretty suggestive: "If I was an itty-bitty girl, I would marry an elevator man—he'd be as good as any—he's gonna go up, I'm gonna go down—we're gonna go up and down together—ain't we gonna have a whole lot of fun going up and down on one another."

The early rock 'n' roll song, "Rock Around the Clock," sounded like a song I used to sing at the Garden. Whoever wrote that song must have heard the version I knew. It started out at one o'clock and continued round the clock.

> I looked at the clock and the clock struck one
> Come on baby let's have some fun.
> Let 'em roll, let 'em roll a long, long time.
> I'm so glad I'm living and I'm so glad that you're mine
>
> When the clock struck eleven, it said, baby, don't stop.
> It's like Maxwell House coffee, it's good to the last drop.

On the nine o'clock verse I'd sing,

> I looked at the clock and the clock struck nine.
> I said, roll over, baby, let's try it from…

I would never sing "behind;" I'd let them think whatever they wanted to think. It usually got a laugh.

Once I was singing "People Will Say We're in Love." The song begins, "Don't throw bouquets at me…" Some joker in the audience yelled out, "Don't worry, we won't." I kept on singing. He wasn't paying me anything and he already had made a jerk out of himself. But there were not many hecklers. There was no violence; people behaved. The gays stayed at their own tables and many straight people who came in were tourists or curiosity seekers, and were probably a little shy. For most people, going to the Garden was daring.

As a general rule, I didn't rehearse. The people in the show did because they had a routine. I would tell the organist what key I sang in and I'd have a rundown on the different acts and then I'd introduce them. I'd often open the show with a song, followed by two acts, and then I'd sing again, and another two acts and I'd sing again. The entertainers would always do a finale but I was generally not included. When it was over, I'd come on and tell the guests about the next show.

One night I was invited to a dinner at the Sessions Club where Louis Armstrong was the guest of honor. I enjoyed his company very much, he had a lot of black consciousness. All the kids at the Garden dressed me up for it. Skippy LaRue loaned me his fur cape and someone loaned me his bright tomato-red dress.

A party of interns and nurses invited me to their table to have a drink one night. They would not believe I was not a female impersonator. My voice is low and I do like to kid around a bit so they kept on saying, "No, you're a man." Finally, I grabbed one of the nurses and took her into the ladies room and it just happened I was having my menstrual period, so I showed her and said, "If I'm not a woman, nature is playing one helluva trick on me!" You know, that woman just stood there and told me she didn't believe it. I sure wouldn't want her to be nursing me.

Our union at the Garden was American Guild of Variety Artists, AGVA. This was a union for the entertainers; the musicians had their own union. We had our union representative who'd try to get new members and we'd have meetings. Some didn't join—they'd say, "What am I getting out of it?" Some people did their own bookings, but it was difficult because the booking agents wouldn't handle you if you weren't in the union.

I usually wore long evening-type dresses at the Garden, and later the mid-calf cocktail dresses, but they were still considered evening wear. I had one cocktail dress that had the stomach cut out of it. Women did not wear the low-cut dresses in 1950 and they did not wear slacks. Some lesbians wore them and some courageous straight women did, but everyone would label them gay. I wore one dress designed with one shoulder off. When I went into the ladies room of Rosellini's 610 restaurant, two women looked at me as though I were a hussy. They thought it was terrible, but that's the way it was in 1950—one must conform.

I knew a lot of gay people then, but I traveled in mostly straight society so I'd hear these comments about the Garden. I think the mix of straight and gay gave the place a certain charge. It made the Garden work, night after night, for ten years.

Black people didn't hang out at the Garden; they had their own places like the Black and Tan, China Pheasant, Elks Club on Jackson, Washington Social Club, and the Sessions Club. When they came to the Garden, it was often to show an out-of-town friend, like a jazz musician, the hot places around town. They were always treated well. In those days, you hardly ever heard of a black gay person; they kept their business to themselves. They didn't advertise like white people did. It's like black people just can't get enough discrimination. I think the black gay people didn't come down because of the stigma.

I think black and white intermixed a lot more in those days than people realize. Most of the after-hours places were run by blacks. Some white women went with black men but they lived mostly in the black area. Black people did not live all around the city like they do now. Seattle had a reputation as the best place for interracial marriages, especially black and white.

I've run into a lot of prejudice in my life but not at the Garden. But when I walked down the street and someone called me "nigger" because I was married to a

★ Wanda Brown sang jazz, blues, and pop at the Garden and was singing in a Seattle jazz bar into the 1990s.

black man, I just tried to keep walking. They weren't hurting me, but were hurting themselves.

Some white women go out with black men just to find out about the black mystique, and the men turn out to be like everybody else. People say the women are going out because the guy's got a big dick. That's so crazy. They have to have an excuse for her even though she doesn't need one. They want to know why one of their own women would choose a black man, so they base it purely on sex. It is the same with the way people talk about gays. They don't know a damn thing about it, so they dwell on sex.

When I worked at the Garden, I met a white girl who became pregnant by a black man. She wanted the baby, but her parents did not. She asked me if I wanted to adopt the baby. Vernon and I were not able to have a child, so we said, "Yes." We were advised not to try to adopt but to just get custody and raise the child. We might have lost the right to adopt because Vernon had spent nine months in prison for a small bag of marijuana. He was caught in a raid of an after-hours club on Jackson Street and the marijuana was found on his dressing table—someone had put it there. During Prohibition, it was understood that in a raid you put your hands in your pockets to prevent someone from putting drugs there. That's what happened to Vernon.

Anyway, I took the woman into my home and cared for her while I faked my own

★ Michael Phelan and his Princess Toulaire performed the "Jungle Dance" at the Garden. "Michael had a beautiful body," LaVonne Bain said. "He'd smear his luscious body with baby oil and Tabu perfume." Phelan gave up boxing, he told friends, because he didn't like the violence, and took up dancing. In Seattle, he stayed with black friends because of discrimination in downtown hotels.

pregnancy and still worked at the Garden. At the time of delivery, I drove her to the hospital and three days later she was driven by and handed her daughter to me through the window. After some tears, she drove off and I never saw her again. Later, I adopted

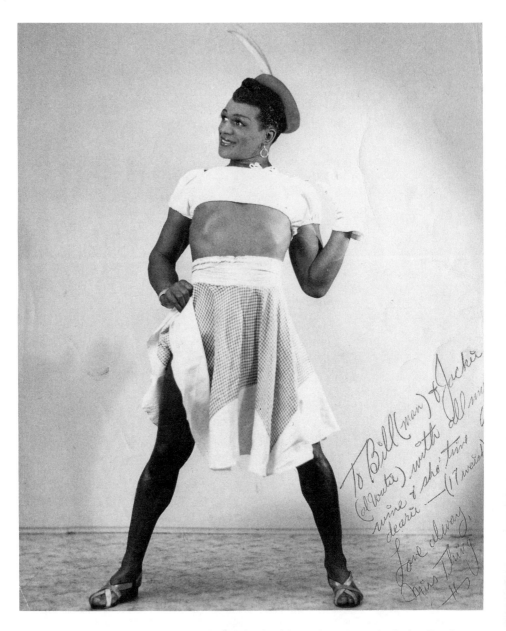

★ Although he was an impressive dancer, Michael Phelan also did comedy routines at the Garden. Here, he played his alter ego, Miss Thing, who sang campy songs and flirted with the audience.

my daughter legally. After Vernon died, I had to tell her in order to properly adopt her. She was fourteen at the time and took it kind of hard, but it all worked out. As far as she's concerned, I'm her mom.

RICKY REYNOLDS

Ricky Reynolds, who was born August 10, 1933, also was known as Ricky Remonde when he performed as a singer and female impersonator. He lives in Minneapolis and cares for his mother. We talked by telephone about his career with the *Jewel Box Revue* and as a performer at the Garden and other clubs.

★

Show business and drag were a part of my life from an early age. You might say I started my career at six months when I played the baby Jesus in a school play. I was always in school plays and experimenting with costumes.

I was eleven when I went into the *Jewel Box Revue*. I literally went to the stage door and asked to be in the show. I was tall, cute, slender, and beautiful and I was a glorious singer. People around me didn't care about age. As long as you carried yourself, no one cared. People would ask me how old I was but they never believed me.

I was with the *Revue* on and off for fourteen years. Then I traveled with *Babe Baker's Ha Ha Revue*, a traveling show based in Hollywood, Florida. It was a big revue, like the *Jewel Box*, but not as well known. They were the only big traveling shows featuring female impersonators.

There were not many Finocchio-style female impersonator clubs in the 1940s and '50s, so any would stand out. I remember the Moroccan Village in New York City, the My Oh My Club in New Orleans, the Ha Ha, the Jewel Box, and the Gayla in the Miami area, the Garden of Eden on Los Palmas in Hollywood, California, and the Paradise Club in Minneapolis.

I loved Doc Benner and Danny Brown who owned the *Jewel Box Revue*. They were dear friends for many years. Danny Brown and I had a pact, which Doc knew about and went along with. No one got a lot of money in the show and I got top wage, but when I got a better offer, I'd leave the show and take it. Danny and I would pick a mock fight and either I'd quit or he'd fire me. We did this because we didn't want others in the show to know. I was a headliner and this would be a big disruption and everyone would have to fill in for me. It was more work for them.

I was primarily a singer, but in those days you did everything. If they told you to hang by your toes in the nude, you did. I enjoyed every moment of it. I was more of an "actress who could sing very well" rather than a "singer who could act." I made people feel what I was singing. I'd sing to an audience of five thousand people like I was talking to them.

I made top money wherever I worked; I demanded it. I always opened with an up tune, a lot of tunes that people hadn't heard, a lot of ballads. I had a number of themes, depending on the show. One song was, "S'wonderful, s'marvelous, that you could care for me."

There was so much live entertainment in those days before television. All the clubs and even the saloons had live entertainment, real singing, and no lip synch. I did not fashion myself after any movie star or glamorous person, I was just me. But when I

★ Not one ray reached these charming ladies thanks to their stylish parasols. From left, Ricky Reynolds, Jackie Starr, and Hotcha Hinton.

first got into the *Jewel Box Revue* everyone helped me get it all together. I was so young I didn't know all those things, but on the other hand I was pretty precocious.

I was to open at a club in Cleveland, but two days before I got there the place was bombed. They said it was the Mafia. Whatever, they didn't want a nightclub in that area and especially didn't want a female impersonator. Well, my lawyer and my agent got together and went across the street and rented the Circle Theatre for me to appear in. It was a beautiful old theater that seated 3,500. The night I opened the place was packed, but people out on the street were picketing. It was unnerving. Just before the show the sound system went out, the audience was getting restless and vocal. I went down to the orchestra leader and said, "We're going to do the show anyway." He got up and announced me and I went on and let me tell you they heard me clear to the third balcony. After my performance I got a standing ovation. The picketers never bothered us again. We were there sixteen weeks, doing two one-hour shows a day.

I was at the Garden for a couple of years. I was appearing in Los Angeles and I'd heard about the Garden and seen their newspaper advertisements, so I gave them a call and they hired me. I was fourteen years old. I bluffed my way through the age barrier. I was there from 1947 to 1949.

I loved everybody at the Garden. We had fun at the Garden and we worked hard.

★ The Garden entertainers were as fascinated as the rest of America with the South Pacific. From left, Billy DeVoe, Jackie Starr, Hotcha Hinton, and Ricky Reynolds.

Everybody put their ideas together and came up with the show. I was paid about $85 a week. In those days that was pretty good money.

I personally had no trouble during the McCarthy era, but I was going with an FBI agent, who was actually working for McCarthy, at the time. His job was to roust out Communists. We never discussed it; he told me who he was up front, but I didn't want to know anything about it.

I've had my share of gay bashing. Once this guy picked a fight as I was leaving a theater. I was a good dancer and a high kicker. I kicked him right where it counted. I cold-cocked him. He left me alone after that.

I quit show business when I was thirty-five, in about 1968. I was appearing at the

Town and Country Club in Brooklyn and Loew's State Theater in New York City at the same time. They helicoptered me from Manhattan to Brooklyn. And then I was rehearsing for a new show as well. I'd get home from Brooklyn at 6 A.M., go to rehearsal at 8 A.M., get a few hours sleep, then go off to do the show at Loew's State. Finally, I just said, "To hell with it, I'm tired." I moved to Hollywood, but eventually I moved back to Minneapolis to be close to my family, especially my mother.

I don't think about sex anymore. I've lost interest. That's fine with me, no more lovers, it's too much trouble. I get my strokes and hugs from people so I'm nourished. I'm fighting cancer and I get radiation three times a week. A twenty-four-year-old aide has fallen for me, but I say, "No, I've gone through that too many times; I don't want a lover. But I love you, I'm flattered, but I just don't want it."

I have no regrets about all those years, not at all, no, no, no, no, no. I wish the world were different, not so violent, more live entertainment. It was so great back then, you could break into show business at so many levels. I like television, but because of it all those places are gone. Yes, I'd love to be twenty again if I had a wish; yes, that would be fun.

If the Garden of Allah were still in business, I'd be there every night. In many ways the Garden represents my youth. Yes, the fabulous Garden of Allah. How we loved that place.

BERNIE CAREY

Bernie Carey had been a hairdresser in Hollywood for more than twenty years when I interviewed him in 1990. Carey, born April 21, 1922, died in early 1993.

★

I was twenty-four when I began working at the Garden as a pop singer in 1946. I was the elegant type, dressed in basic black and white, dangling earrings, turban, and chiffon. I was known for my attractive legs.

I have always liked to sing. You might describe me as a high-pitched tenor. I'd sing several numbers, usually sophisticated nightclub songs, then have some fun paraphrasing lyrics. One of my lines was "I'm a big girl now and I want to be handled like one." There was seldom any heckling. If there was anything like that I'd say politely, "Won't you please come up and sing with me?"

I loved shoes. The higher the heels, the better. I bought all my women's shoes at Rhodes department store on Second and Union, then I'd decorate them with sequins and rhinestones. I bought my dresses there also. Since I bought only basic black or white, it was not difficult to convince the saleslady that I was buying for my mother (but it just so happens that I am her size). I had a lot of experience looking at clothes I knew would fit me so I'd ask the saleslady to hold it up so I could see it on me in the mirror. Under my clothing on stage I wore nylon hose and a panty girdle. I never shaved my chest and wore high fitting dresses, but I was never able to tuck my private parts between my legs like some did. Hotcha and some of the kids at the Garden had

★ Bernie Carey in 1977. After the Garden closed, he owned a hair salon whose customers included Hollywood stars.

electrolysis to remove body hair, but I never did. I loved good perfumes, the most expensive possible. Shalimar was my favorite.

I left the Garden of Allah for an eight-month tour of the Beige Room in Los Angeles, Ann's 440 in New York, Chi Chi's in Palm Springs, and Finocchio's in San Francisco. When I returned to the Garden after the tour, I got $75 a night, a hefty increase.

Sue Carol (Alan Ladd's wife) was my agent for awhile and I made a screen test for 20th Century Fox. Sue wanted me to go to acting school because things were looking good. But other things were pulling on my life. I was raised a Catholic and for two years I went to a seminary. I became convinced that what I was doing in show business was a mortal sin. The Church still hasn't got the message. Drag had become boring so in 1952 I became a hairdresser at Rhodes department store, and later I operated a salon at Frederick & Nelson department store.

Then for the next twenty years, my hair salon in Hollywood served such stars as Ginger Rogers, Lucille Ball, and Kathryn Grayson.

DOROTHY BROWN

Dorothy Brown, born November 4, 1920, played the Garden's organ in its honky-tonk tavern incarnation, as well as during its time as a female-impersonator cabaret. I interviewed her at her home in Spokane, Washington, about a year before her death.

★

I have been a professional musician, playing the pipe organ, for fifty years. I played the Wurlitzer at the Garden of Allah and at the Lyons Music Hall [a nearby cabaret, mostly a hangout for sailors].

Rehearsal day was Monday. We'd rehearse so long we didn't even get to eat. We had to rehearse all those different acts for three shows a night. The first and third show were the same and the second was different. Every couple of weeks the show changed; you can see how much work it was to keep it all going.

Francis Blair was the producer of the shows in the two years I was there. Earl Steves, a drummer, died in 1989 as a very old man. Most of the other musicians are dead. Jimmy Baker, I heard, lives in Alaska. Gene Smith and his wife, Happy, played the Garden, but they're both dead. Gene played the organ and Happy played the drums. Ray Watkins was the drummer there for years; he worked with Ronnie Bowers on the organ, and they're both dead.

The Garden was the only gay bar I played in. Of course, everybody had a crack at that, I mean playing for shows was not a lot of fun. It was hard work and there were so few pipe organists who could do both—play for shows and play for dancing between the shows. After the Garden, I swore I'd never play for shows again, they just tear you apart. It's very nerve-wracking. Each performer knows his or her act so well and you're supposed to do it as well as they do, and you get so little rehearsal to get it down. It just makes you sweat, and if something goes wrong, who gets it? You! But I got along real good with the group at the Garden and we had a lot of fun. Their revues followed the seasons and holidays and they would base their costumes on that as well as a million other themes.

Nattajon danced the "Moth and the Flame" around a burning candle on toe. He was in drag, a ballerina outfit, and he wore a wig. He had said to me while we rehearsed that it had been a long time since he'd danced on toe. In the show, we went through the whole orchestration. My back was to him, and I had a mirror so I could see behind me. But I was concentrating on the music, and didn't see that he was trying to signal for me and the drummer to stop. He had broken his ankle, but he finished the number.

One time Wanda Brown, the emcee, said to me in a calm voice, "Don't panic, but if it gets hot under your feet, jump." There was a short somewhere and sparks were flying under my feet, but I kept right on playing and finished the show.

KIM DRAKE

Kim Drake, a female impersonator, at first sang torch songs in Garden shows, but later became one of the emcees. Born November 9, 1932, Drake was still in his teens when he became part of the Garden's history. I talked to him in Seat-

★ Kim Drake tried the Air Force after playing the Garden and lasted only eight weeks; a sergeant saw him buffing his nails and applying clear polish.

tle's Rainier Valley neighborhood as he recovered from a heart attack and heart surgery.

★

In October 1948 (I was fifteen), Ricky Reynolds picked me up and took me to the Governor Hotel where he was living. He thought he had some "chicken" but I was already experienced. I became the darling of the female impersonators at the Garden. Ricky, Jackie Starr, and Robin Raye fawned over me and one day, when I was sixteen, they decided to play a joke on the Garden's management. They taught me a song, dressed me, put on makeup, got me some false ID and I performed on amateur night. They offered me a contract right there. I had already quit school and I was drinking too much and definitely needed something to do. So I had a job at the Garden when I was sixteen and stayed in the show off and on for four years. I was a little like Rosalind Russell or Jane Russell when I was on the stage.

My first night at the Garden was a smash hit although I was scared to death. Ricky, Robin, and Jackie were rooting for me, though, and that gave me courage. I loved the applause. I sang "Diamonds Are a Girl's Best Friend," which became my theme song. Later my theme was "To You Sweetheart, Aloha," which I'd sing to some handsome guy in the audience.

I would wear a strapless full-length dress with a fitted bodice and a full skirt so it gave me a chance to move. I tried a few times to wear a hobble skirt, like Marilyn Monroe, a very tight dress with a slit at the bottom, but it was too hard to walk in heels so we'd make the slit higher. In those days we didn't have panty hose; we had nylons with garter belts to hold them up.

The dressing room was about twelve feet square with a long table with mirrors and lights like any stage dressing room. You had five people dressing with all the costumes so it got pretty hectic. We'd arrive a little after six in the evening and start the makeup and be ready at 8:30. It usually took an hour or two to get everything glued into place. This was in the early evening and as the show went on you were only back there if you had a long time between numbers. If you didn't, we had a small costume place curtained off near the stage for a quick change. Between shows we might drink with the customers. We would camp and scream with them but we couldn't dance with them.

The atmosphere in the dressing room was congenial; we talked about what was going on, gossiped a little, but you're very busy. You're trying to get your face on and those eyelashes on straight and eyebrows take a lot of work, and the beard, and then you have to get psyched up for it. It's like shedding this person and building that person and getting into the essence of the person you have become.

In the dressing room you begin to focus on what you're doing in the show tonight. What have I got that's witty, what song am I going to sing tonight, who is my latest love, or who's broken my heart. You try to get the emotions going. Now do I want to be bitchy or witty or melancholy? Do I want to be Mae West or Greta Garbo?

I did my own makeup. You'd look for a base as natural to your skin color as possible and put it on heavy enough to cover the beard. We'd block out our eyebrows with makeup and flesh-colored tape and paint a new eyebrow above the natural one. Or we might shave off the eyebrow completely. We put rouge on the cheekbone to highlight it. Most drag queens are pretty good makeup artists. They know what works out there at the back of the audience, but they can look ghastly up close. I paid about $35 for my wigs at first, and later up to $155. They were expensive.

We had no scenery or sets at the Garden so we had to create all illusions with lights and music. The lights were controlled at the bar. There were about seven spots above the stage in two or three rows and a follow spot at the bar where they could change the colors. We never got paid to rehearse so we'd have to work it out before the show if we wanted more amber or blue, whatever. Rehearsal was Monday night after the last show and the Garden was closed. But then we didn't have anything to do the next day anyway.

The music would start an hour or so before the show for dancing, then organist or

★ T. C. Jones, an impersonator who often performed with eight chorus boys, headlined the Garden and other nightclub bills around the country.

musicians would take a break. That would give the audience time to get fresh drinks and settle down before the show began.

Dorothy Brown played the organ and you were always safe with her. I read music so I wouldn't change key but drags that didn't read would sometimes change key in the middle of the song and Dorothy would always hear it and change her key accordingly. All the music was set and we would interpret it. We loved Dorothy because she would go with you. Sometimes we'd be so loaded we'd go all over the place, but usually would get back at the close of the song.

The show would start with Dorothy Brown on the organ playing eight or sixteen bars from my theme song, "Diamonds…" Then the house lights would go off and the stage lights came on and I would come prancing out there with my head held high. I would do or say anything to sell the show. I'd say to the audience: "Good evening, Ladies and Gentlemen. You know who you are, but all your reputations were ruined anyway the minute you walked down the stairs. So you might as well sit back and relax and enjoy the show because we are going to enjoy it. Welcome to the gay, glamorous, gorgeous Garden of Allah where boys meet girls and sometimes you can't tell the difference."

I had no set patter, everything would be spontaneous, ad libbed, you fed off the audience. I'd patter away and let them know my middle name is Available and I was husband shopping. ("I'm yours for a price. I'm Available.") I'd come downstage and look over the audience to see who I could pick on or who was going to give me a bad time and who I could have some fun with. With my hand mike I'd turn to some guy in the audience and say, "Now on my right is Miss Chi Chi Gay. She walks, she talks, she'll even get down on her belly and wiggle like a reptile but step back boys because she bites." I'd turn to another and say of his basket, "Hmmm, is that for real honey or is it cotton." We kept it funny, light, and tried to get them friendly and laughing.

I'd always pick on a man in the audience but not in a mean way unless he heckled me. I never picked on a woman unless she also heckled. I'd take out my falsies and say, "Alright, I've taken mine out, let's see you take yours out." Or I'd take mine out and say, "These are great. I scrubbed the floor and washed the car with these today and I'm wearing them tonight." You had to react right away to a heckler; you couldn't let them get away with it. Most straight men don't heckle as much as you'd think. A lot of them at the Garden would make a big deal about getting their picture taken with a drag queen smooching on him. I think straight men enjoy getting a blow job from a drag queen. They have the fantasy of it being a woman and all the tenderness and expertise a guy can give. As emcee I was always throwing out the line: "A hard man is good to find, but us Seattle girls get the other kind."

Then I'd introduce an act, usually a singer. Sometimes Lee Leonard, Bernie Carey, or T. C. Jones would be there. Jones was only there three weeks because the Garden couldn't afford him. First off, he had to have star billing and Francis Blair hated that. No one was a star except Francis. T. C. Jones always traveled with eight chorus boys. She'd be doing her number and the boys would be dancing in the back. He would end his number by lying across the eight of them and they'd take him off with his gown dragging across the stage.

At the Garden we all got the same salary, $125 a week (ribbon clerks got only $35 a week). So you didn't have to climb each other's back to get more money at the Garden. You did at Finocchio's. We all had our specialties so there was no stealing of numbers or material. But in a distant city I might use a line or two far from the one I heard it in.

We really worked at our art and we saw it as an art form. We worked to be the best we could be. Drags today don't do anything. They say they work at it, but they don't give themselves a chance. They don't know anything about yesterday's drags —Jackie who? or Julian who?

I drank a lot in those days. Everything was a party and we were all drunks. I'm still a drunk at sixty though I don't drink anymore. Then I felt bad about myself because being gay was sick and a drag queen was even sicker. Alcohol was one of the only ways we had to cope with society. When I drank I could block all that out and when I went in drag I felt the real me come out. I created my own fantasy; that's how I survived.

I got my first reefer from one of the musicians at the Garden. He said, "Smoke this and it'll make whatever you're doing easier." I didn't particularly like it; I was into booze and speed. There was a stigma against marijuana use, but people popped bennies like vitamins. I don't remember any grass in the dressing room, but we did have speed and whiskey. If we were caught that would have been a closure for the Garden. Fortunately, the inspectors never came back to the dressing room.

There was a lot of police harassment in the mid 1950s. There was a beat cop in Seattle we named Hitler. He would arrest a drag queen in a minute. They'd take you up to jail in drag and throw you into a cell and tell the other prisoners to rape you and some would. I always connected with the biggest guy there for protection and would say, "I'll be your dolly." Even out of drag you could be lined up and suspected of being a fruit, anything to depersonalize, demean you. If you were in drag, you'd have to hire a taxi and rush into wherever you were going.

I also played in San Francisco, New Orleans, Detroit, etc. I followed T. C. Jones at the Beige Room in San Francisco. That club opened as a challenge to Marge Finocchio's place. She had power with the city because her place was such a huge tourist attraction and had a monopoly on tourist drag bars. The Beige Room broke that monopoly. The difference between Finocchio's and the Garden was that Finocchio's paid you according to the draw. For a season I traveled with Francis and Kenny Bee to Alaska. We took the boat to Ketchikan and worked ourselves up the coastal cities to Anchorage and then to Fairbanks and Nome. We made a ton of money but we drank it up and whored all along the way. You gotta keep the men happy. We'd always say, "For a little extra money, we'll give you a special show." We were all whores but Francis was too much of a lady to admit it.

In 1950, I thought I'd go straight for awhile and joined the Air Force. I lasted eight weeks. One night the sergeant saw me buffing my nails and putting on clear polish. He said, "Men don't do that." I said, "Well, the men I know do." I was just too nelly for them. I got an undesirable discharge. "Fraudulent enlistment," they called it. I marked no in the block for homosexuality. The sergeant and I had a little romp in the hay before he turned me in.

I just ignored my discharge. My parents weren't happy, but they weren't happy about me working at the Garden anyway. When I interviewed for a job I'd just put down that I was never in the service and if they asked I'd tell them I was gay. It never caused me problems. Years later I got something from the Air Force asking if I wanted my discharge changed. I didn't bother. It never caused me not to get a passport or any clearances I needed.

If you only went with each other in those days you were a ki-ki queen. When you were a queen, you were a bottom. If your partner was straight trade or gay trade, they were the top and you got screwed or you blew them. The emphasis was on picking up a man, not another fairy. Queens looked down on ki-ki queens. One day I went into this bar and a handsome blonde marine came in. I was about to make a move on him when this dizzy queen came in and sat down next to him. He tried to pick him up at which point the marine slugged him, knocked him down, and he rolled under the pinball machine. I thought my God, that could have been me. The marine got up to leave and came over to me, smiled, and said, "Let's go." I was completely surprised, but of course I went with him up to his room in the old Kennedy Hotel. He said, "Well, I guess I'll take off my clothes and go to bed." I said, "I'll leave now." He said, "Well, don't you want to lie down with me." The marine took off his pants and underwear and rolled over on his stomach. He had the roundest, most voluptuous hairless butt I'd ever seen. I almost fainted. He reached around and laid his belt across that beautiful butt and said, "I want you to spank me with the belt, then fuck the hell out of me." I was offended. I grabbed my coat and said, "I'm sorry, but I don't fuck around with ki-ki queens," and left.

In my years at the Garden, I didn't have sex unless it was for money. One of my regulars was a man of about sixty who had a large bed in the middle of his room. He wanted me to wear a garter belt with black panties, gloves, and face makeup, but no bra and wig. All he wanted me to do was walk around the bed and strike poses for forty-five minutes and he'd give me $75. I guess he was turned on by the Frifty Thrumpky, the old carnival image of a person who was half man and half woman, or hermaphrodite.

In the early 1950s, I met Mr. Right who convinced me I was living the life of Mr. Wrong. So I gave up drag and the night life and began to teach professional ice skating.

PEEWEE NATTAJON

The Garden of Allah was home to two Nattajons, one an elderly actor with years of stage and screen experience whose specialty was acts in which he played two persons at once, "half and half" acts; and the other a teenager named Bill Plant, born September 24, 1929, who took the stage name of Peewee Nattajon for female impersonation. In this interview, Plant talks about both his stage persona and the older man who was the inspiration for some of his work. Plant is a minister and founder in 1971 of the Awareness of Life Church in Renton, a Seattle suburb. Nattajon has resumed drag performances; he and his straight son, both in drag, perform for Seattle charities which feed homeless persons.

★

At sixteen I got married, went into the U.S. Army when I was seventeen, and to the Garden of Allah when I was eighteen. Bobby Talbot, a gay woman I was stationed with at Fort Lewis, introduced me to the Garden. I took right to it. The Garden was not elaborate like Finocchio's in San Francisco, but the talent was as good. The Garden was not a drinking place because they did not allow drunks in order to protect the tourist trade.

I lived at the Governor Hotel—it was a dive. Jackie Starr and several kids at the Garden lived there, too. Most of us lived on the third floor. The second floor was more transient. A lot of prostitutes and a couple guys who hired themselves out as personal escorts and a madam also lived there. The Japanese landlady didn't care as long as you paid your rent and didn't cause trouble.

Kenny Baker, one of the organists at the Garden, talked me into going on the amateur show on Wednesdays. If you won you got one week's booking on the show. I won and I was thrilled and went on the amateur night ten or twelve times after that.

I was basically a dancer and my stage name was Peewee Nattajon. You might say I was the protege of Nattajon, Lee Leonard, Jackie Starr, and Robin Raye. They just latched on to me and decided to make a complete transformation. They'd get me down and smear Nair all over me even though I had little body hair to begin with, and then they'd get out the cosmetics and go to work on me. Jackie would say, "You little son of a bitch; you're just the cutest little thing. You've got a face like a baby's butt." They did all my costumes and make-up and just fussed and fussed over me. I never did know anything about either one and I never really learned. I loved all that special attention.

The first time I went on stage I was scared to death. Kenny Baker was on the organ and everytime I danced close to the organ he'd play with one hand and grab me on the butt with the other. The audience loved it. Kenny said he did it just to liven up the show. After awhile I gained more confidence. I was small and cute so I could wear the highest heels and those enormous Carmen Miranda fruit-bowl hats and still not look like a giant in drag. My Carmen Miranda act was very successful as well as my roller-skating act done in a short skirt. I also did an Aunt Jemima and actually sang a song.

One day Jackie and Lee gave me a curious look and decided they were going to make a stripper out of me. Lee said, "What are we going to do with his testicles?" Jackie said, "We're going to make ovaries out of them." Jackie made my G-string. It had a thin elastic string that would go inside the skin, in the folds. My testicles would go up into the sockets and my penis would be pulled flat between my legs by the G-string. The larger the penis the harder it is to pull off. After awhile, it would become uncomfortable and it was hard to sit down and could be quite painful.

I called my striptease act, "The Dance of the Veils." My bra could be taken off because my A-cup falsies were glued to me. They were filled with water and when I danced I could hear them sloshing around. Jackie would only allow so much water in them because too much weight would break the seal and they would fall off. We taped our chests to bring out our natural cleavage.

Nattajon was one of my mentors. We stayed friends right to the end. When he couldn't work anymore, it seemed everybody turned their back on him. I didn't.

He was fifty years old in 1945 and had been in show business for thirty-five years, since 1910. He was a character actor; he didn't sing or strip or go into drag per se. He played in all the important supper clubs in California and did character parts in thirteen Hollywood movies, such as *Beauty and the Beast* and *The Picture of Dorian Gray*. At the Garden he did a series of half-man, half-woman acts: "Beauty and the Beast" and "The Sailor and the Woman." He would have a split costume, one half woman and the other half gorilla, sailor, etc. There was no vocal, just music from the pipe organ, just acting, but it was so real. You really believed there were two people there. For instance, for his sailor and woman act, he'd sit on a bench with his legs crossed, one arm around himself, then act out this scenario, of course very suggestive, but the illusion was terrific because it was so well done. The woman in the act had half of a blond wig with hair three feet long.

Nattajon designed and made all his own costumes. He was an excellent seamstress. He was secretive and maintained an air of mystery. He could be cold or flamboyant at the Garden, but on the street or in public he was eccentric, but always a gentleman. He was an actor, a little outrageous and proud. He was always kind of a miser. He'd walk across town to save a nickel. He saved his money, but in the last five years of his life he was ill and spent all his savings and lived in an inexpensive hotel room in Los Angeles on social security.

We lost touch for awhile, but connected later when I was a private nurse for George Burns at M-G-M. Gracie had just died and George hit the bottle. It wasn't easy, but I helped control his drinking while he did the El Producto cigar commercials and a movie, *Girl Across the Hall*. Somehow my picture showed up on a television show and that's how Nattajon found me. I visited him in his messy hotel room where he'd lived for years. He was so thin. I guess he was denying himself food in order to save money; he was always afraid of running out of money. He had nothing but fifty years of costumes rotting in his closet. I helped Nattajon through the last years of his life. He said, "You can do anything you want with me, but don't put me in the ground." I had my dear old friend cremated.

I got married to a gay woman and we had a son in 1944. When my wife came home from the hospital, she handed our son to me and said, "Here he is. You wanted him so you can take care of him." She got a job as a mechanic and I stayed home and raised our boy. Later I married again to a woman who knew I was gay and we also had a son. I got rid of all my photographs and keepsakes from the Garden. I also sold or gave away all of Nattajon's things. God, I wish I'd saved the pictures. But those were the 1950s. You had to be careful about incriminating evidence.

At one point at the Garden if you were in drag you could not mingle with the customers at their tables. Jackie Starr got away with it, because he was the star. The drags usually sat at a table in the corner and customers could come over and talk to them, but only the women could sit down with them.

Back in the Garden days we didn't have the freedom that came later. If you want to walk down the street in drag today you can. Back then you had to hide those things, especially in the McCarthy era. You could be thrown in jail easily. I don't know how many times I was thrown in jail on a charge of soliciting—just for being gay. Then you could be molested, raped, beaten by cops in elevators. I had to leave town once. I was beaten by the police so I filed a brutality charge against the officer. I sued the city but they turned the tables on me. Some lesbian friends took me down to Portland and we went fruit tramping for awhile. If I hadn't gotten out of town,

★ Peewee Nattajon and his son, both in drag, perform to raise money for a Seattle homeless charity, Strand Helpers.

this cop would have had someone beat me up real bad. Later they found out he was a crooked cop. He had this city official beat up who turned out to be an undercover cop. He not only lost his job but an opportunity as he was running for chief of police at the time.

KENNY BEE

Kenny Bee was one of the Garden's emcees, sometimes in camp drag and often as a straight male, and sang and danced in camp drag routines. He lives in Kokomo, Indiana, where he moved in the early 1960s to care for his mother. He performed steadily until the late '80s. "Kenny Bee in drag never tried to look good," Countess Estelle said. "He could come out on stage looking like death warmed over and the audience would just crack up."

★

I was born March 24, 1914, in Delaware, Ohio. I had nine sisters and two brothers. My parents were very loving. My father died when I was young and my mother encouraged me in everything I did. My mother danced in the line with the Ziegfeld Follies and I think I got my talent from her.

I didn't come out until I was eighteen—I was a late bloomer. When I was twenty-five, I told all my family at one gathering. There was absolute silence. One sister said, "I knew it, I knew it." But they all loved me so they accepted it.

I attended Ohio State University and majored in music and dance. I was preparing for a straight singing career. After Ohio State and all through the 1930s, I was a vocalist for several dance bands. My first job was with the Hal Denman band and then Artie Shaw bought my contract and I traveled with him for a couple of years. I was the only person to sing "Indian Love Call" swing-style. I was also with the Louis Peneko band and Buddy Rogers band. Buddy was gay and married to Mary Pickford, who was twenty years his senior and who loved all the gay kids.

For awhile I tried my luck in Hollywood and got a part in *Flying Down to Rio* with Ginger Rogers and Fred Astaire, then played the son of Marie Dressler and Wallace Beery in *Home Town Boy*. Later, I made a screen test for Marjorie Main and Percy Kilbride, who said, "That's the man we want to play our next to oldest son" in the Ma and Pa Kettle movies. I loved Marjorie Main and the rumors that she was difficult on the set are not true. She loved the gay kids and Percy didn't care. "Live and let live," he said. A few years ago, they had a Ma and Pa Kettle reunion and Marjorie Main made sure I'd be there.

During the Second World War I was an Army company clerk and later a secretary for a three-star general. I was in New Guinea, the Philippines, and Guadalcanal. The general was an old family man and tolerant of gays, and there were a lot of them. He'd say, "I like all my girls." I made first lieutenant.

After the war, I resumed my nightclub career and my agent, Ted Pearlman, steered me to the Garden of Allah. I was there for a total of fifty-seven weeks. It was the greatest place of all, more fun than anyplace I've been. We were all friends and there was no professional jealousy. When I was emcee, I'd always say, "We're all stars here; we're all equal." I got $100 for three shows a day, six days a week.

I was a solo act when I went to the Garden. I sang, danced, and did emcee work in both camp drag and as a straight male. I would usually appear in camp drag for the first show, straight male for the second, and camp drag for the third. When in camp drag, I always pretended I was beautiful and that would really amuse the audience. When I was emcee, if someone questioned my beauty I'd say, "What are you looking at? You could get this way, too." I came out on stage insulting everybody. I'd say, "Ladies and Gentlemen, I call you that because I don't know what the hell you are!" With my stony face, the more I insulted them, the more they loved it. I only did a Prima Donna once, in Columbus, Ohio.

In my "pregnant woman" act, I'd have a pillow stuffed under my dress and come out on stage dragged down, stonefaced, runny socks, baggy blouse, and sing my version of "I'm the Talk of the Town." The words were: "I can't go anyplace, can't show my face; Everyone knows I'm going to have a baby; I'm the talk of the town. I sent out invitations to friends and relatives, announcing my wedding day, then he ran away, left me this way, so everybody knows I'm going to have a baby. I'm the talk of the town." I was pathetic and the audience howled. Then I'd turn my back to the audi-

★ Kenny Bee combed the thrift stores for outrageous costumes for camp-drag routines in which he often was paired with Francis Blair.

ence, whip that pillow out and toss it behind the curtain so fast no one knew I did it. Then I'd spin around doing a tap dance and be completely flat and sing, "Please don't talk about me when I'm gone."

I met Lee Leonard at the Ballyhoo speakeasy in Columbus, Ohio, in 1931. He got me into comedy and helped put together my "pregnant woman" act and my striptease. In my strip, I'd come out wearing five coats, blouses, and dresses, and take them off one by one. The audience would scream, "Take it off! Take it off!" Then I'd get to the last piece which would be long, red underwear with chicken feathers under the armpits, a swinging bicycle lock on my ass, and a large mouse trap over my crotch with a rubber mouse in it.

Sometimes dressed in a tuxedo or a suit and tie I would just sing a song straight, such as "Don't Take Your Love from Me," "I'm in the Mood for Love," "My Blue Heaven," "Embraceable You," "I Can Dream, Can't I?" "Rain," "You Made Me Love You," or "You Made Me What I Am Today." I also did risque songs, such as "Meet Me at the Pawnshop and I'll Kiss You Under the Balls," "Who Lit the Fuse in Mrs. Murphy's Tampon," or "Get Off the Stove, Mama, You're Too Old to Ride the Range." Sometimes Frank Carlburg would come up to me and say, "Kenny, you got dirty." I also did risque versions of popular songs, such as "My Blue Heaven":

> Last night, oh boy was I tight,
> I stumbled into my blue heaven.
> I turned to the right and switched on the light,
> There was a hell of a fight,
> Right in my blue heaven.
> A rolling pin hit me on the chin,
> A chair or two,
> When I awoke my jaw was broke,
> Both my eyes were blue,
> Just my wife and me, her old lady made three,
> They beat the hell out of me,
> Right in my blue heaven.

One day in 1947, Carlburg said to me, "Why don't you and Francis Blair get together and do something in the show." We put together some acts combining talk, song, and dance, both comedy and straight, but with a lot of emphasis on comedy. We'd practice at Francis' place, my place at the Governor Hotel, or at the Garden when they were cleaning up in the afternoon. We'd also go up the street and practice at Lyons Music Hall. Harvey Lyons would play the organ for us.

We combed the Goodwills for old clothes from the Victorian era. We found some dresses and hats from a huge pile of old clothes and even some bustles in the back of the Goodwill store at the Pike Place Market. We searched for months for the old button-up shoes from the 1890s and we finally found them. We even found some original 1890 umbrellas and swimsuits. Hotcha made some of our costumes; she was an excellent seamstress.

Francis and I were a great team. I was like Jerry Lewis, the comedy from left field, and Francis was like Dean Martin, the straight man. Except when we were doing straight acts, I was always dressed wrong. Francis would play either a Dame or a glamorous Prima Donna. In our act, she was the Prima Donna being constantly exasperated by my antics but determined to get on with the show. I'd say or do something wrong or get out of step, we'd have a mock argument, and I'd go to the bench on the Garden's south wall and sit there quietly while Francis sang her song. But once in a while I'd look under my dress or fuss with my panties, which came down past my knees, and the audience would burst into laughter. That of course would seem to upset Francis and she'd have to struggle to get the show going again. Or I'd take a tit out and look at it and then stuff it back in again. One night I threw it at her. I did all this with a straight face. No one could crack me up. It's a matter of making up your mind—nothing was funny, you didn't crack a smile. I was like Buster Keaton.

But I could always break Francis up. She'd see something I did, and she'd crack up. But she was good at playing the straight man. But Francis could do nutty things, too, like take the rubber ball padding from her brassiere and bounce it on the floor, or take a cherry from her pocket and say, "This is my cherry. I didn't do anything with it today either," and throw it into her purse.

In our "Gay Nineties" routine we played it both straight and comedy. Francis would be in a beautiful Victorian dress and I would dress in either my white or black tuxedo. But sometimes I'd be in a dress, too, and we'd do a camp routine. We might be singing "Let Me Call You Sweetheart" and I'd purposely forget the words or go off key and Francis and I would get into a mock fight and start insulting each other. That wouldn't be hard because those old high-button shoes would be killing our feet, especially when we did a soft-shoe dance as part of the act. Sometimes we'd do a Gay Nineties routine in bathing suits from Goodwill.

Our "Two Old Bags from Tacoma" routine was a Garden favorite. We'd dress in our Gay Nineties outfits as two old gossipy women insulting each other as well as the audience. But we never said bad things about Tacoma because many of our customers would be from there. The audience applauded wildly and we had lots of curtain calls.

Our dialogue was always about men. I'd say something about one and Francis would say, "How do you know about him?" and I'd say I'd slept with him, too. We argued constantly about which man liked which of us best, who was most successful with men, who was treated better on dates. We'd just go on and on with this bitch fight, or fight about which of us was prettiest, youngest, or smartest. One of us would say to the other, "Don't try to hide behind makeup because you were born ugly and nothing can be done to hide nature's mistake." Sometimes when Francis was waiting in the wings, I'd carry on about how miserable she was: she was so poor even Goodwill was too expensive and that's why she dressed that way. She's just starting out in show business, I'd say, and she's to be pitied, so please feel sorry for her and give her a nice round of applause.

In our "Hillbilly" routine, we wore old country dresses, long braided wigs, tattered hats, and sometimes no shoes. We joked back and forth in hillbilly slang, clog danced, and sang one of the old-time songs like "Silver Threads Among the Gold." We always sang the songs straight; we never made fun of the music. Sometimes I just screwed up by singing off key or forgetting the words.

We did our comic "Apache dance" in mini-skirts. It got rough. We threw each other all over the place to a wild Spanish song played on the Wurlitzer. Francis would pick me up, whirl me around, then let me go flying across the stage. I knew of course how to land. In the old days of vaudeville, we'd have been called a "nut act." We got pretty crazy.

We also did our straight soft-shoe and tap-dance routines to songs like "My Blue Heaven" and "Singing In the Rain." I'd be wearing a tux and Francis would be in high drag holding a Victorian umbrella she got at the Goodwill store. We might begin by singing two choruses of "Me and My Shadow," do a slow tap, then sing the last half of the song. Sometimes we'd do a fast tap that was always a crowd pleaser.

We had a great time and we really worked hard. Every other week or so we'd put together a new show and of course we'd always be nervous the first show, but then you could do a show a thousand times and still be nervous. But once you got out there you'd break away from that nervousness and do your best. I would try to block everything out of my mind except what I was going to do in the show.

The dressing rooms at the Garden were hot in the summer. I didn't wear too much makeup because we had no air conditioning and with the hot weather and lights, makeup would run. One entertainer put on too much makeup which began to melt and she looked like a zebra.

Francis and I toured all over the West Coast, Midwest, and Alaska. We were a very successful team and we made money, but I spent it as fast as I made it. We were very successful in Alaska. I'd be out there looking like the wreck of the Hesperus and would flirt with some guy in the audience. I'd be acting like I was the most beautiful thing on earth and the guy would usually go along with it. People would throw coins at us and I'd say, "Fold them, please," so they'd throw dollar bills which Francis would stuff in her bosom. I'd lift up my dress and stuff the bills in my rolled up stockings. We got good tips. Those Alaska boys loved risque humor. Some places we each made $250 a week.

When we were in Chicago, an agent helped us get a booking at Finocchio's in San Francisco. At Finocchio's I used my old line, "We're all stars here," but some of the kids didn't like that because they considered themselves the stars. I couldn't stand the cast there. They wouldn't speak to us and were so jealous because we were such a hit. I finally went to Mr. Finocchio and said, "I'm sorry. I'm an entertainer, but not like this." He offered more money. We said, no, and left. He said, "You're the only ones to quit here." I said, "Well, we're the smartest ones as long as you have those bitches."

Francis and I were a team for nine years. Francis didn't smoke or drink; he'd get on me for smoking. He was motherly. He wanted to be The Star and he was good to everybody.

After the Garden closed, I cooked at the All-Nations Cafe in Pioneer Square and performed at night at the Double Header tavern, doing my old Garden routines. I also sang with local dance bands. In the early 1960s, I went back to Kokomo to take care of my mother, and after she died I continued singing in straight clubs, doing comedy only occasionally. I worked steadily until 1989, and still do some emcee work and singing. I enjoy my free time now.

ROBIN RAYE

Robin Raye, an exotic dancer and stripper in Garden shows, lives in a rambler which he and his late wife found in the 1960s in Rohnert Park, a town fifty miles south of San Francisco. He was starting to remodel the house, partly as a way of recovering from his wife's death, when I conducted the first interview. He was also renewing his gay life for the first time in thirty years, and was optimistic about that.

★

I was born October 28, 1925, and raised in Montana. My parents were wonderful and I had a good childhood. I learned my gardening and other skills from them; that's the way you did it in those depression years, you raised much of your food and did every-thing yourself. I learned all about sewing and quilt-making from my mother and I have put that skill to good use all my life.

Later we moved to Seattle. I spent some time in the navy then studied costume design at the University of Washington. In Montana I studied dancing and acrobatics.

I was twenty-two years old when I met a guy in Seattle in 1948 who asked me if I wanted to go to the Garden of Allah. When I saw it I couldn't believe it, all these gay people and female impersonators. On a dare I went on the show on amateur night and did my first strip. Dottie Carol, a friend, put me into the business of female impersonation and dancing. Dottie was a buxom little lady who sang parodies and did some emceeing at the Garden. She helped me with my makeup and we found a nice old velvet dress at the Goodwill store in the Pike Place Market, and underneath it I wore underthings and stripped down to a G-string. I tucked in my genitals. I stripped to "In a Persian Market." I won first prize which was a week's booking and got $30 or $40.

My Garden of Allah debut set a pattern that lasted twenty years. I became a pro-fessional exotic dancer from that night on. Female impersonation was the farthest thing from my mind but after one show it became my career. My off-stage nickname was Boo Boo; I think Lee Leonard gave me that name. Later, when I worked the Gar-den I got $85 a week.

I was basically an exotic dancer and stripper. I sang a little bit in the finale show at the Garden and rapped with the audience. I'd do bumps, grinds, shimmies, belly rolls—the whole thing, but I put comedy into it. I was doing, you might say, exotic burlesque with comedy, but not slapstick. For instance, I'd stop dancing and rub the back of my leg softly with my other leg. It didn't mean anything, it was one of those hundred little kooky things I'd throw in for comic relief so they wouldn't concentrate just on my maleness. Or I'd have some straight shots of v.o. whiskey waiting for me at certain tables and before I drank the shots, I'd do comedy things like pat it under my arms or on my crotch or pour it on the floor just to have fun. Jasmine, also a stripper and my wife-to-be, used to get so mad at me because I would be drunk by the time I got back to the dressing room.

When I stripped I used songs like "Let Me Entertain You," "The Stripper," "Song of India," "Dawn on the Desert," and "In a Persian Market." When I did exotic material, I used "Song of India," or "The Saber Dance." My character numbers were jungle, harem, Hawaiian, Jewish, Hungarian, voodoo, etc. With "Seven Veils," I used seven different colored thin gauze veils. I also did a geisha girl, oriental things, a gypsy girl. Later I danced with the Deva Ja Dancers doing oriental and Bali-type numbers. I also performed with Tito Puente on his show.

There was one song I searched years for. It was a song that Nattajon used in his "Beauty and the Beast" act and had a very eerie kind of drum beat. Nattajon was very secretive and cut off all the titles on his sheet music so not even the musicians would know what he was playing. I learned eventually the song was "Dawn on the Desert." I used that in my voodoo number. My music was what you could buy on the sheet-music market and then you'd run into someone who could write in a drum or a horn part.

The whole thing in stripping is the tease. I think if I had a hero it would be Gypsy Rose Lee. She was the master of the tease without ever just tearing your clothes off. My dad took me to see Sally Rand at the Rivoli Theatre when I was in high school. I saw Ann Corio at the Palomar in the early 1940s; her parrots flew to her from the balcony and took off pieces of her costume as part of the tease.

I would rehearse with the musicians first and I'd time my strip to the music. Then I could give certain cues or I'd say, "Let's go home," which meant let's wrap it up. You learn to work the way the music is phrased. Depending on the club, the strip would last ten, fifteen, or even twenty minutes. It was hard to keep it going for that long, but I'd do things in between, more and more teasing.

I'd do burlesque-style stripping. You might say I was impersonating a burlesque stripper. In my later years, I just did regular strips, not "characters." It was a lot easier and I'd get as much response.

My garments would be a large skirt and a smaller skirt, a cloak around my shoulders, and gloves. I'd usually wear mesh opera hose. My shoes would include heels or soft flat leather slippers or no shoes at all. I always wore my own wigs. These garments were made with little hooks and eyelets so they could be easily removed. Of course, you'd unhook or remove something without being obvious.

Fortunately, I did not have to wear full body makeup. Jasmine did because of stretch marks but I was blessed with a clear, smooth complexion.

I'd arrive at the Garden about two hours before curtain time. In the winter it could be cold, and hot and stuffy in the summer. The Garden had three makeup stalls and an old common plank floor. I made all my own costumes. I had a woman make one

★ An unusual publicity photograph showed Robin Raye as an exotic dancer and as a man.

of my costumes once but it just didn't work. My costumes had to do what I wanted them to do. They had to be convenient for me, like easy to put on and take off, and move well, etc. I had knockers filled with bird-seed. I used many kinds of fabrics, whatever the mood called for. I made all of Jasmine's and Lee Leonard's costumes for years. I also made costumes for Carol Wallace, another friend of long standing, who was the famous emcee at Finocchio's for many years.

I made lots of costumes for my good friend Billy DeVoe, the "Park Avenue Hillbilly." Billy always dressed elegantly and sang cute little numbers with that Oklahoma twang. Billy was a singer and a master of ceremonies. He liked to sing the livelier tunes; I only heard him sing a ballad once. One of his songs was "Music, Maestro, Please." We called him Modine Pineknot. We saw him when he was appearing at Finocchio's in the late 1960s, then we lost track of him. Judy Garland had seen his show and told him she wished she had his voice. She brought a bottle of champagne to the dressing room and sat and camped with Billy and the other impersonators. "God, I wish I could look as good as you bitches," she told them. We did Billy's wigs when Jasmine and I were in the wig and costume business after we retired from show business to raise our daughter Valerie. We shared apartments and did many shows together, and Billy and Jasmine and I were good friends. I was recently reunited with Billy.

How we tucked away our genitals was always the gossipy discussion at the tables. Jackie Starr and I did it basically the same way. We pushed our testicles up into the sockets and a pouch held our penis back between our legs so it would be flat looking, then tied back by the G-string. Jackie as I understand was not small, but during a strip he was as flat as a pancake. It took some doing. He would strip right down to a rhinestone clip. He was more fleshy around the waist than I. I pretty much taught myself how to do it that worked for me, and of course the way you moved and held yourself, and the type of pants or G-string that you were wearing created an illusion that there was nothing there. As we moved with our testicles in the sockets, our testicles never got pinched.

The Garden was a wild place when it got going and we had a lot of fun there. It didn't have a good reputation. "All the fruits went there" was the local gossip. I can remember thinking it had this awful tile floor, the kind they used in latrines. Being in one of those old buildings added greatly to its reputation as a dive. Of course, now I see that floor as gorgeous and the old building which I thought so ugly was a treasure. But Victorian architecture was not "in" in 1948. We were modern; Victorian was the old people's world.

What I was doing never bothered my mother. She'd come and sit through all three shows at the Garden. She loved it. She'd come to other cities where we were playing. You couldn't take off the makeup between shows so I'd powder down and put on men's clothes and my mother and I would go out in public to shop or eat and of course people would stare at me, but my mother never hesitated to say that I was her son and be proud of me. My brother never mentioned my career or saw any of my shows and I'm sure he was embarrassed but nothing was ever said. My sister was okay and the rest of the family never objected, but it wouldn't have changed my life anyway.

In 1950 I worked at Finocchio's. In many ways this was a message that you had arrived on the gay-tourist night-club circuit. It wasn't necessarily the highest you

★ Robin Raye's clear complexion and sophisticated style made his striptease numbers popular at the Garden.

could go, but it was the most famous. I made $150 a week at Finocchio's; that was about the most we made in those days. Mr. Finocchio was okay, but Mrs. Finocchio was on an unrelenting control trip. To be in her good graces everyone on the show had to say goodnight to her and say goodnight to Paddy, her dog. Well, I wouldn't so she called me on it one day and said, "I hear you've been saying things behind my back." I said, "Mrs. Finocchio, I haven't said anything about you and your husband.

★ Jasmine, an exotic dancer shown here, and Robin Raye were married in 1958; the marriage lasted until her death thirty years later.

You're not interesting enough for me to talk about." "Well!" she said; she reeled back in her chair.

I was there for another six months and I never spoke to her. My friends were aghast and said Mrs. Finocchio would have you for another six months if you'd play her game, but I said, "I don't care. I don't want to stay in this toilet." Mrs. Finocchio made millions off the drag queens. I don't think she liked gay people, but she certainly knew how to use them. At Finocchio's you could not mix with the customers. All you could do is sit back in the dressing room and fight with each other.

I was with the *Jewel Box Revue* briefly in 1951. The money wasn't good and I really didn't enjoy doing a big drag show. The productions were wonderful and it was kind of fun to be in that, but it was monotonous, the same people and routines for a whole season. Someone left the show and Gita Gilmore suggested me so I met them in Erie, Pennsylvania, then we went to Syracuse and Rochester and then to Detroit to a big theater but it bombed because the police wouldn't allow them to advertise—dumb, stupid homophobia. It was a big production. Mickey Mercer was the star impersonator and she sang "Donkey Serenade" and came on stage with a live donkey. After three days they closed the show and went back to the Jewel Box Club in Miami.

They let go anyone who was making big money on the show because business was terrible. The sea was full of Man-of-War, stinging jellyfish, and the tourists stayed away that year. We used to do a two-and-a-half-hour show for four people. In the front of the club they had a gay bar so they wanted us to get into men's clothes, take off our wigs but leave our makeup on and go to the gay bar and hustle drinks. It was the dumbest thing. I could see the writing on the wall so I left and went to New Orleans.

I went back to the Garden, met Lee Leonard, and we teamed up; our separate acts complemented each other. A lot of clubs where we worked only wanted one or two acts so it was easy to go into a club as a novelty act and fill the whole bill. He emceed, told jokes, and sang straight and risque songs. Lee had a great voice, a masculine voice, and he was very good at singing the blues. Lee and I traveled in separate cars together for years, doing our own acts but on the same bill. We got along fine because there was no conflict, but he got rid of anyone who sang and told jokes on the show like he did. He could really be a bitch. We spent two years in Oregon alone. We traveled all around the state. At Coos Bay, people stood in line to see us at a club that held three hundred people. Lots of places were jammed every night. Then we traveled all around California and in many states east.

Lee and I (and later with Jasmine) played straight clubs almost exclusively. We never played the gay circuit except on a rare occasion. We performed at some of the best clubs in the U.S., including Alaska and Hawaii, Canada, and Japan. They loved us in Japan. In Japan we played the Golden Okasaka, a huge and elaborate night club of unusual beauty. We played the Jewel Room there and another club in Tokyo, a tourist place like Finocchio's, always packed with Japanese tourists. It was the Hanabosha Club, a world-famous club and the place to go in Tokyo. Lee got the gig through an agent.

Lee wanted to play the Magic Inn in Seattle, a straight club that did not hire gay acts. Everybody said, "You'll never play the Magic Inn," but Lee bugged the owner so much he finally agreed to give us a week's booking. We drew the biggest crowd the club ever had and our engagement was extended and we played there every year for years. We outdrew Sophie Tucker at the Magic Inn. After each show Lee demanded payment. He had been burned too many times. We worked together on and off for years but sometimes I would go on the road alone.

Lee Leonard was a master at working the audience. Lee would always find someone he could bait and some remarks would fly and off he'd go. That's a lot of what made his act because he had an answer to everything, he was never stumped. He used to say, "You know what a heckler is? It's a baiter and you're a master of it." The audience would really respond and he could go on and on. His show would often go way overtime. I, however, never got that rough.

I met Jasmine at the Pioneer Hotel, a theatrical hotel in Denver. Lee Leonard and I were together then and the first place we worked was the Inferno, across the street from a brand-new club called the Tropics, where Jasmine was headlining as an exotic, which includes stripping. This was around 1954. Jasmine and I didn't meet again until around 1956 in Spokane, where we were both working. We started going together and got married in 1958. Lee gave our marriage three months, but it lasted thirty years.

We hit it off right away. Physically we meshed, our careers meshed, and we both knew what we wanted, a home and family, and we worked toward that end. We were completely devoted, especially after our daughter was born.

I was thirty-three when we married and I had been around the gay block, but I felt I gave up nothing. Of course, there were temptations. Jasmine must have been tempted, too, but we satisfied each other physically and certainly emotionally. We made a commitment and we stuck to it.

When Jasmine and I were married it was fine with Lee and me for awhile, but I didn't have as much time to spend with Lee. Jasmine and I just went ahead on our own when we did things and didn't ask Lee, so eventually we drifted apart. Lee felt left out and there was some bad feelings. I have never seen Lee since around 1962 but in 1968 he gave me a call from the hospital where he was having his sex change. Later he came to San Francisco with his bosses at the Gay 90s in Minneapolis where he was working. Jasmine had stopped dancing and was working as a cocktail waitress at the Chi Chi on Broadway in San Francisco. They brought Lee (now Liz Lyons) to see her and they had a good visit. I couldn't make it at the time for some reason. I never saw her as a woman and I never talked to her again. I have no idea where she is. I've tried to find out but no one knows.

Jasmine, Lee, and I traveled together for awhile doing our separate acts but it just didn't work so Jasmine and I began to go on the road together. I was always a female impersonator, just like I was at the Garden of Allah, but I would often be billed as a novelty act, which was a way of making it legitimate for straight people to justify seeing. Jasmine and I had our own separate acts so there was never any conflict. Sometimes we'd be billed as Mr. and Mrs. Exotic, or Guess Who's Who?—that sort of thing. Sometimes I'd take off my wig but not always. I never ran across any rules and regulations about what was acceptable for a female impersonator to do on stage. I didn't have to identify myself if I didn't want to. We never worked the gay clubs and as a novelty act there wasn't as much scrutiny.

When our daughter Valerie was on her way Jasmine did not want to raise her in such a hot/cold climate as Minneapolis, although that city was good to us. We rented a truck and moved everything west. It was the first time I'd driven a truck. We stayed for awhile with Jasmine's brother looking for houses to buy. My wife walked into this one and said, "This is my house and we're not moving anymore." We paid $14,000 for it on June 17, 1961, with nothing down.

Valerie was born on July 7, 1961. You might say she was born in a suitcase. She was on the road with us from five weeks on. We'd go on the road for four days at a time and come back home on weekends and I would help Jasmine's brother paint houses. Valerie was a super kid to travel with, but we'd always have to find a baby sitter and attend to all the requirements of a growing child. After five years of this Jasmine and I decided to retire from show business and raise Valerie. I did my last show in 1968. Jasmine and I then went into the costume and wig-salon business for the next twenty years. I am a grandfather now and close to Valerie, but Jasmine died in 1988. My friend Carol Wallace said to me when Jasmine died, "Don't do what I did when my wife died. I sat around for three years and didn't do anything."

I had a lot of fun times when I was single but I did enjoy working with Jasmine because you were with somebody and it all had more of a purpose, although I wouldn't give up those times at the Garden of Allah when I was single for anything. Many a night Wanda and I would work Chinatown after the Garden closed and for a few bucks we'd perform at one of those after-hours bottle clubs. It was fun and we knew everybody. We knew all the madams and all the hustling girls and all the rounders, and they knew you and treated you well. There was always parties then, we had a lot of fun and I enjoyed it all. I don't think I have any regrets—perhaps only that I didn't save some of that money but I wouldn't exchange it for anything. I never felt I was missing out on my gay sexuality. Jasmine and I were always so involved. Maybe my outlet was being in drag, but I never went out on the street in drag and I never carried on behind Jasmine's back. I was true to her.

Jasmine had good sense. I am more thankful for her good sense now that she's gone than I did when she was alive. Jasmine had an aneurysm and after three months in the hospital, she had a massive heart attack.

I'm retired now. I don't have a big social life because the majority of my time is spent on my quilt business. I get out to quilt shows but I live from day to day. Some days I work hard and others I take it easy, work in my garden, or on my house. I think about going out more, but I think, "What am I doing, cruising at my age?" Who would I look for? You're always comparing to what you had.

I've thought about selling my house and moving close to my daughter, but I just can't make that decision. Houses are more expensive where she lives and my house is going down in price. But I have my garden which I absolutely need, and I have room for my grandkids and daughter when they come to stay. Life is about change and when the time comes to move, I'll be ready.

chapter 7

SKIPPY LARUE'S STORY

★

ONE

IMPERSONATOR'S

JOURNEY

TO THE

GARDEN

OF ALLAH

Skippy LaRue, who performed as a female impersonator at the Garden of Allah, lives in a mobile home in south Everett, a blue-collar city thirty miles north of Seattle. He still works at a gay bathhouse in Seattle, reputedly the oldest one in the United States. His capacity for organization and his frequent contact with others who knew the Garden made him one of my best sources. His story includes details of his life before he became a female impersonator at the Garden of Allah because I believe it is important to know the unusual, and often unacknowledged, routes by which some men became female impersonators. His story ends with an account that suggests that many impersonators, like those who worked in the *Jewel Box Revue* and at the Garden, also found outlets for their talents in carnival work.

THE BLACK SHEEP AND MADAM HARDTIMES

★

I was born in Port Arthur, Texas, on April 5, 1921. My father was a boilermaker, but he also bootlegged whiskey. My mother ran a house of prostitution where we all lived. I think my father was a kind man, but I guess I think that because he only beat me once. I disobeyed him and went to a girlfriend's house. He came over with a stick and beat me all the way home while he called me a "fuzzy-headed little whore." My mother beat me every day and I have physical problems to this day. My family didn't want me; they shipped me off to an aunt until I was five. I was the black sheep and was disowned. I talked to my nephew thirty years later and he'd never heard of me.

Everyone called my mother Big Mama, including me. At first, I didn't call her mother because I didn't know who she was. She never wanted me and didn't like me because I was a change-of-life baby. She said, "If you'd been born a girl, I'd have sewed you up." My brother hated me, too, and was mean to me. He got the best of everything.

My family used to tease me a lot. I'd be doing homework and my brother or my mother would turn off the light and I'd go into a panic and they'd laugh. Today if I try to sleep without a light I get sick. Even now I react if someone touches me while I'm asleep. My mother caused that. My mother would come in my room in the middle of the night and be mad because I read the newspaper before she did, and didn't put it back together exactly the way it was. She'd take the light cord, double it up, and go to town on me.

I started drinking when I was five years old. My parents would sit me up on the bar at a party and bet that I could drink a glass of whiskey down. They always won their bet. I was five the first time I got sick from drinking. We used to drink beer instead of water because we were too far out of Port Arthur to be on the water line. In the summer, the water from our cistern got foul, so we drank homebrew and homemade wine.

I've had gay feelings from a very early age. The first time I did anything sexual I was nine. A woman who lived at our house had a son about fourteen and we had to share the same bed. One night he had an erection and he shoved my face down there and shot all over me. Then he gave me a quarter. I thought, "Hey, this is okay. A quarter is a lot of money"; the local prostitutes were only getting a quarter. The next night he did it again, but I held it in my mouth, then went into the bathroom to spit it out and rinsed my mouth out with water. The next night I just took a glass of water to bed with me.

The first time a man kissed me I was ten years old. Oh, God, that was wonderful. They had curling irons in those days and I'd get one of the girls in our house to curl my hair. I think my parents had their doubts about me from an early age. But there was no doubt at age eleven when I got expelled from grade school for hustling merchant seamen. I'd hang around a merchant seamen's club downtown and hustle the guys. I'd have my hair curled and I'd look just like a little girl. I'd say, "Do you have a match?" That would get the conversation going and I'd get a dime or a quarter or some cigarettes for giving a French job [fellatio]. That's when I got kicked out of school. That was pretty much the end of family life for me.

Later, my parents sent me off again to live with an aunt in Louisiana. A young neighbor man who took care of his mother was so handsome. Once I stayed at their place too late and his mother told him to walk me home. In the woods, he asked me to sit on his lap, then started kissing me. He was so affectionate and I was thrilled. I gave him a French job. Another time I stayed overnight in his bed. He went into the kitchen for some butter, greased me up, and just rammed it in. God, it hurt! I thought I was going to die. After awhile, we had a nice affair going. He gave me a lot of affection and I would have done anything for him. But I was shipped back to Port Arthur and the nightmare began again.

I cried a lot in those days, just about every night for a long time. I'd lie there alone night after night and hear that lonely train whistle blow when it passed through town at midnight. I planned to run away. Then I met an older boy, Jimmy, who I had tricked with and he took me down across the tracks to where the whorehouses were and introduced me to a madam called Evelyn Hardtimes.

She had a large and nicely furnished whorehouse in Port Arthur's red-light district. When the guys came off the ships, they'd pass the black "shotgun houses." Every house in a whole block had just a tiny living room, kitchen, and bedroom. The toilets were outside, so they used "peter pans" in the house. All the black girls lived in the "shotgun houses." In the same area were the finer houses like the one run by Evelyn Hardtimes.

Soon, I left home and moved in with Evelyn and worked for her for a couple of years. I'd tend bar and do other chores, but when a customer wanted a boy it would be me. Men who liked to fuck boys in the ass were called wolves. To Evelyn, a twelve-year-old boy was no different than a twelve-year-old girl. At that time, many girls became prostitutes at twelve or thirteen. Other madams at other houses called me from time to time. Since I was the only boy, I'd charge double—50 cents. If a customer protested and said he could get a girl for a quarter, I'd say, "But I'm the only boy."

I thought I was the only one like me in the world. I didn't even know the word homosexual; I thought the men who liked to fuck me just liked to fuck boys. Later I learned that I was a queer or a pansy. I was pretty flamboyant and looked like a little girl. I wore men's clothes but they were like satin shirts and I painted my fingernails and bleached my hair blond. When I was twelve, people on the street turned to stare at me. People used to bet on whether I was a girl or a boy.

The madams got me dates with judges, lawyers, police, doctors, military officers, and executives as well as seamen and a little bit of everything else. I was trustworthy and dependable. I was known all around and even when I went to Seattle years later, the madams had heard of me.

All the cops knew I was a male prostitute but they didn't bother me because Madam Hardtimes paid them off. I liked the young men best but I saw a lot of older men, too. That didn't bother me. I guess I just liked the attention and loving they gave me. I felt wanted and I was doing it on my own.

Very few girls turned French tricks in those days. If a guy came in and asked for a blow job, the girls wouldn't have anything to do with him. Once in awhile one of the girls would complain that I got too many tricks, but I'd say, "Well, I'm the only one sucking dick around here!" I was called Dorothy, the French kiss expert. A lot of guys came into houses to get French dates because they didn't want to ask their wives to do it. French was a novelty then. I've been in many threesomes, but I've never had sex with a woman. I did not turn any black tricks because the houses were segregated in those days. If a white man wanted a black woman, he went to the black houses. If a black man wanted a white woman, he could find one in the black houses.

I was eighteen when I met my first gay person. Cecil and I became good friends and he introduced me to all his gay friends. This was my first awareness that there was a community of people like me. I was working Madam Gracie's house then, so after the bars closed and on Sundays, my new friends began to hang out there. I was tending bar and turning tricks at the same time. Gracie liked the kids and they and the girls really enjoyed each other. We had so much fun talking and laughing about men and trading stories.

For the next fifteen years I tried working at a few straight jobs—drugstores and delivery work, but I always seemed to wind up in a dress. I guess I was a hustling girl. The first time I went in drag was when a girlfriend fixed me up and got me a job as a carhop at the Sweetheart Roadhouse. I served customers in their cars and got them to pump dimes into the juke box. I'd stand there and drink with them, but if anyone wanted a date, we'd work something out for later. I was strictly a French date, unless the man knew I was a man and was okay.

I learned as a carhop that I was more successful as a female hustling girl, so drag became a matter of survival, but at the time if it had been possible for me to become a woman sexually, I would have had it done.

GOING "STRAIGHT" AT THE GARDEN
★

During one of my periods of going straight I hired out of Houston to work at the Boeing Company in Seattle. I did not go into the service during the war because of an ear injury my mother caused. Boeing paid me 72 cents an hour. Later, I worked at the Blackball ferry dock lunch counter in Seattle for several years.

Jimmy Kelly would tell me about this great place called the Garden of Allah, but I didn't go to places that only sold beer and wine. I went to the after-hours places where you could take in your own whiskey. Then I met Jackie Starr at a party in West Seattle and we became good friends. Jackie was hired by her agent to come here and perform and like myself she liked it so much she stayed. I lived in the old Governor Hotel on Fifth Avenue and rented the large dining room and kitchen they made into an apartment. Then Jackie moved into the Governor and first thing you knew it was full of gays.

My apartment was a huge space and I only paid $10 or $15 a week as I got in before the rent freeze. Our landlady didn't care as long as we paid our rent. After an all-night party there would be soldiers and sailors crashed all over the hotel lobby.

I began to know so many people who went to the Garden of Allah that eventually I hung out there too. I really began to like the place. I went there every night.

They talked me into joining the show. I wasn't really into show business, but I said I would.

For awhile I did shows at the Garden every week. I was a hootchy-kootchy dancer and sang risque songs. I worked at the dock, but on my days off I'd go down for rehearsal and start drinking, do the show, and continue drinking. I sang a lot of songs like "Hot Nuts" and "Around the Clock" and I'd make up lyrics as I went along. ("Now you see that man with the shirt of brown. Well he's got the hottest nuts in town. Nuts, red hot nuts, you get 'em from the peanut man.") Jackie helped me with that and my wardrobe and makeup, which I never knew much about. I toned down all my songs at the Garden, but on the road later or at an after-hours club, I'd do some really dirty ones. You could get by with singing the dirty lyrics at the Garden as long as no one heard them. You'd use another word, or whisper the word, or be silent and let the audience fill in the word.

Jackie showed me how to make a G-string out of a cloth table napkin. It was strong, not like a regular G-string. Then you put your testicles up into the sockets very carefully. You take your penis, wrap it in half a Kleenex, then tie the Kleenex with elastic as tight as you can, pull it back between your legs and up between your cheeks even tighter, make a loop just at your tailbone, then pull the elastic around your waist and tie it at the back. The string gives you the lips. Then you've got a pussy. In the carnival, we called it "gaffing up." I would wear a cape to cover the elastic. When I first started my Madame Fifi act, I thought I'd stay all tied up between shows because it would take time to tie back up. I learned not to do that because I began to hurt like hell and my parts were black from lack of circulation.

The dressing rooms at the Garden were so small we didn't hang out there between shows. We'd put on barrel dresses, which we could slip into easily, and sit out front at a table reserved for the entertainers. Depending on whether there was a vice officer around, we could mingle a little with the customers at their tables. Patrons could have their pictures taken with the stars. Sometimes we'd stay at the Garden after it closed and drink and talk. It would be real quiet in the building and the rats would run along the top of the wainscoting.

When the taverns closed, we kept partying at bottle clubs which were open all night. Through the late 1940s and '50s, there were several hundred bottle clubs in the city. A few catered to gays, but the gay kids mingled easily in any of the clubs. Most of the after-hours places were bottle clubs, although a lot of them sold liquor from under the counter. One night just before a raid, the bartender put twelve bottles on our table and said, "These are yours." When the police came, we claimed the bottles so the club wouldn't be charged.

In the last years of the Garden, I rented several houses around the city and ran one bottle club at a time. Then, after the Garden closed at night, we'd all go to my house. We told the police it was a party house, but, of course, it was our version of a bottle club. Customers brought their own bottles, but I had bottles to sell, lots of food, and a spare room if somebody wanted to trick. I wouldn't let in strangers who came by cab. The police were my patrons, but I had to pay them off only once.

★ Skippy LaRue
first performed
at the Garden
in 1947.

When liquor by the drink came in in the late 1940s, the after-hours places began to die out. I stopped working at the Garden and went on the road with the carnival with Hotcha and Jackie.

HIDE, HAIR, AND PUSSY
★

Hotcha had been involved with the carnival for many years and in the early 1950s talked Jackie and me into joining the girlie show on the Art B. Thomas Carnival. Crowds were thinning at the Garden. Jackie was five years older than Hotcha and

★ Jackie Starr, shown here in his trademark fur, taught LaRue the techniques of impersonation and stripping.

I was five years younger than Hotcha. Hotcha and I have been partners one way or another for forty years so I traveled along with her and she paid me out of her salary.

In those days carnivals had terrible reputations. If you were a carny, you were immediately labeled flim-flam. We'd go into a town and because we were carnies they'd switch the menus and we'd have to pay three times the usual price for a meal.

Jackie, Hotcha, and I were on the line at the girlie show with several straight and gay women, all strippers—Lucille, Terri Moore, Hi-C, Melanie, Yvette, etc. Sometimes Jerry Ross joined us on the line. He was a good stripper and went by the name Sherry Lee. He also did the sideshow attraction "Half Man/Half Woman, a Freak of Nature."

★ Jackie Starr and Skippy LaRue were close friends for forty years.

Jackie went by the name of Lotus Lee and I was Skippy LaRue except when I was Mademoiselle Fifi, a one-man girlie act.

Of course, the patrons never knew we were men; they'd have killed us! All the people on the carnival knew but it was okay as long as you did your job and didn't cause trouble. But we were cool; we lived in drag but never acted like dizzy queens. We had our fun but we were expected to be professional. Carnival people had a certain tolerance for the differences in people. They'd say the carnival scene was the last resort for people who did not exactly fit in with the rest of society. You got to know a lot of people in the carnival business—in a way, it was a family. You could walk into any carnival anywhere and always see someone you knew or worked with. Once Hotcha, Jackie, and I visited another carnival and met some black queens in their girlie show. We invited them to come and visit us but they said, "Oh, no, we can't do that; they don't like queens." Jackie, Hotcha, and I looked at each other and practically said at once, "Well, what do you think we are?" We all had a good laugh about that one.

Carnival life was not easy. Setting up and tearing down and then traveling to the next town was exhausting enough, but then you had to do your thing. In the few months the carnival was active you had only one shot at it. You've got to get the money when it's in front of you. We'd sometimes be shaking our asses at 6 a.m. They'd come around and wake everyone up because there would be people on the fairground.

Some of those small towns way out in the Dakotas or somewhere were only fifty or sixty miles apart. It got so the marks knew the games better than we did and called us by our first names. Some of the games on the line were not exactly legitimate. They were called "flat stores."

But before a carnival came to town a "patch man" (lawyer) would go to the police as an advance man and discuss the different games and attractions (like the girlie shows) and determine just what will be allowed and the price of it. Sometimes the Texas Rangers would come around the carnivals in Texas and take an attitude. They'd walk down the midway and see a game they didn't approve of and not only close it down on the spot but tip things over. They were very powerful and all the carnival people feared them. In a sense they were sort of a vigilante committee and that's very scary.

There were always cops and detectives at the carnival snooping around to watch for anything going on that wasn't agreed upon. At one of our towns two plain-clothesmen were hanging around because they suspected one of the girlie attractions called Madame Fifi was prostituting. One of them was talking to the other about my show with Jackie and Hotcha. He was talking about Jackie and me doing our sexy dance: "…and then the mother gets into that act!" He thought Hotcha was our mother. We all got a big kick out of that but Hotcha was furious.

It was hard work but we had a lot of fun doing the girlie show. We got along well with the straight girls on the line. Sometimes we'd do five or six shows a night. The first show would be for both men and women and that, of course, would be pretty tame. After the "blow off" (when all the people left the grandstand show and flocked to the midway) we'd do our second show called "The Blow"—men only. We'd spin a sexy platter on the phonograph and do a strip tease down to nothing. We'd wear a panel of cloth around our shoulders which hung down so us boys could partially cover our small breasts and fake it. In these strip numbers makeup does a lot and you are moving so fast the customers didn't know what was going on.

Our third show was called "The Ding" or "Hide, Hair, and Pussy." It was X-rated and for men only. We really got down. The men were not concerned about breasts; for this show they came in for one thing only—pussy. We'd start off by singing a dirty song, do some dancing, and mimic eating each other out, and gradually build up to taking off our clothes. Hotcha got really wild and did things like smoke a cigarette from her navel. She could twist around in some way and cause puffs of smoke. She'd also tape her penis and hide it in the folds of her fat stomach and smoke a cigarette from her pussy, which she could also fake. This would really get the men going. Jackie, Hotcha, and I and the girls would be stripped down to nothing and let the men comb the hair on our pussy. We'd say, "The one who combs the hair on our pussies the best gets a souvenir." We would be all tucked in and taped and it would appear to look like the real thing. By this time the men were so horny they'd believe anything. They'd be combing away and we'd say to one of them, "Well, it looks like you did it just right," and we'd let him pull out a hair from our pussy with his teeth. We'd say, "You can put it in your wallet or put it under your pillow or you can jack off—I don't care what the hell you do with it, but know that you have a souvenir from my pussy."

One time Hotcha, Jackie, and I got busted. I was scared to death. We could have gotten twenty years back then for wearing clothes of the opposite sex. That was a federal offense. If a woman was busted for doing that kind of show she'd have been fined $250 and six months in jail, but there was no law on the books against a man stripping in front of another man. When the sheriff went out of town for a few days his brother-in-law arrested the three of us. They didn't have any quarters for women in the Port Hueneme jail so they took us to Oxnard [California]. Hotcha said right off that she was a man but Jackie and I didn't. We were called into the police chief's office. He leaned back in his chair with a smug look on his face and looked us over. "So, you're men," he said; "prove it." We hoisted our dresses and showed him our penises right there. His eyes widened and his mouth fell open.

Word had gotten around so there were a lot of people and reporters at the station. This was the hottest thing that happened in Oxnard in a hundred years and everyone was just dying to get into it. But to the police it was very embarrassing so they wanted to shut it up fast. Finally the chief said, "Just get the hell out of town!" They let us go. Of course, we were to leave town immediately but it was Thanksgiving and we all had a big dinner planned. We weren't about to miss that so we just changed into men's clothes and stayed a couple more days.

For awhile the carnival played Everett, Washington, but the crowds were really scarce. Sometimes we'd do a show for only a few people and for our third show sometimes just this one guy showed up. He was only twenty and extremely handsome and so sweet. It got so we'd look forward to him. His $20 would almost be the only money we'd make in an evening. There'd be four or five of us in the show and only this darling man to play to. We'd shower him with attention and let him feel our pussies and we'd kiss our fingers and touch the head of his penis and generally be sexy for him.

One of the attractions in the carnival sideshow was the African Dunk where you throw a ball and someone gets dunked in water. In the carnival we were working at the time it was called Mabel in the Bed. For awhile I was Mabel (in drag) and was on salary. I was laying on a bed behind a wire screen and someone aimed a ball and tried to hit a target. Hotcha was the front man and got the people to buy three balls for 25 cents. She'd say, "Try to knock Mabel out of the bed. Watch her legs go up in the air and her pants fly off!" I'd land on a mattress and show a little leg as I fell out of the bed. Hotcha could really bring in those customers. Some guy hit the target and I fell out of bed twenty-five times in a row.

Once they didn't have anybody to work the Electric Chair and they cornered me and showed me how it was done. I was screaming and hollering while they dragged me in because I was scared of that damn thing with all that voltage going through you. They said they didn't need a siren or a microphone because people began to flock in to see what the screaming was all about. So I became Miss Electra. I looked like Elsa Lanchester as Frankenstein's bride. With that electricity going through me I could cause sparks, light up light bulbs, cigarettes, and torches. The emcee would use someone's car keys and sparks would fly when he dropped them in my hand. I was to return them to him the same way but I forgot and handed them to him and it shocked the shit out of him.

But not all was work when we were on the road. In one town, Jackie met a straight guy who was queer for high-heel shoes. The next night after our show the guy wanted to go out again, but that night Jackie was wearing flat-heel shoes and I was wearing high-heel shoes. Jackie said, "All you have to do is take your heels and drive them into his chest." I said, "Well, that's okay, I can do that." He knew we were men. When we got to the motel, he wanted Jackie to watch as he laid on the floor and I dug my heels into his chest. He said when he was a kid, he was very shy and his teacher used to sit him up on her desk and he always looked down on her high-heel shoes. I just dug down into that chest and it must have hurt like hell, but he liked it.

chapter 8

THREE HEADLINERS

★

By the time I became aware of the Garden of Allah, several stars of the shows had died, leaving behind only the vivid memories of those who performed with them or watched them from stageside. So in this one chapter, it was necessary to use my own voice to place three of those departed stars—Francis Blair, Hotcha Hinton, and Jackie Starr—in the spotlight. Each had a riveting performing style and personality that left indelible impressions on those who knew them at the Garden.

FRANCIS BLAIR

Kim Drake's best memories of the Garden of Allah are of the moments when he, as emcee, could slash away at Francis Blair, the comic, the Dame, "out there in that camp, ragmatag stuff from the Yukon."

"One night," he said, "Francis was exceptionally nasty to me and I introduced her as a rare treat for the Garden of Allah guests, the last in captivity, one of the original logs skidded down Skid Road to her brothel on Post Street. Francis Blair has the log marks on her ass to prove it."

The fight between Drake and Blair started when they met. Drake, a mouthy newcomer, challenged Blair's statement that he was then twenty-three. "Twenty-three! But you were singing to my father at the Spinning Wheel sixteen years ago." Blair was furious. He told Drake, "You bitch, you be sure to keep your makeup on your side of the table." The long-running spat hints at the tensions between the sexy young impersonators and the older men, infinitely polished in performance, but showing and resisting their age. On stage, Drake would betray the conflict with comments echoing both empathy and derision: "After all, at her age, and if you'd been on as many vaudeville circuits as she has, you'd be wrinkled too. If you can't find IT, you can use her wrinkles."

The bitchiness was okay for the comic roles, but when Blair did his star turns, Drake's lips were sealed. Blair had been a stellar Prima

Donna in Seattle since the early 1930s, and he continued to play that role after the Garden opened.

Francis Blair, like Jackie Starr, was an experienced pro in the Garden days. Drake was right; Blair was thirty-three years old when the club opened. Starr, who was two years younger, learned his work in Chicago and New York; Blair learned his craft in his native city of Seattle. More than anyone else at the Garden, he was Seattle's own. He worked steadily in Seattle cabarets and burlesque houses in the Depression years, honing natural talents for comedy and impersonation. Singing was his strong suit at the Garden, but he also worked dances into his routines, and could do a mean strip. Behind the scenes, he also produced shows and designed costumes. His penchant for organizing things later led him to take an office in the performers' union.

Blair was a striking woman, friends said. For a time, so he didn't have to use wigs, he let his hair grow long, unusual in that day, then contrived ways to conceal it under hats when he was on the street.

Blair was named Charles Schultz when he was born February 8, 1913, in West Seattle, now a neighborhood within the city of Seattle. In his early teens, Blair wore dresses he had pulled from a trunk full of women's clothes, and rode streetcars around the city with his friend Rita Kelsey—"fooling everybody," Kelsey said. He, his mother, and brother "seemed to be going it alone," Kelsey said. "For awhile we were just like brother and sister." After Blair began working at the Florence Theatre, part of the Seattle-area John Danz theater chain, she saw him less often. Kelsey added, "I had pictures of Francis in drag, but my mother would steal them and put them up on her wall, so I'd have to steal them back. She thought Francis was just great."

Blair's love for drag probably continued unabated, although the next report places him in the chorus line of the Rivoli Burlesque Theatre in downtown Seattle in the 1930s. Blair danced as one of the women in the line, but in the dressing room was separated from them by a screen. It was fairly common then for young male dancers to augment their wages with work in drag in the burlesque theaters. Since some of the women also were gay, there was an easy rapport on the line.

Kitty King, who also danced at the Rivoli, remembered "a young guy in the chorus line" who wanted to borrow a very expensive man's suit which she had altered for herself. "He looked at my suit and just drooled. He said, 'Kitty, I have a date tonight and he's going to take me to a fancy place.' I let him wear it, but the date got funny with him and tore the suit off him. He almost had tears in his eyes, he felt so bad. I didn't ask him to replace it, he was just a kid, making only $25 a week."

Kenny Bee and Francis Blair sometimes were the Fred and Ginger of the Garden of Allah. Bee in a tuxedo and Blair in high drag with an elaborate parasol might sing "Me and My Shadow," do a slow tap, then wrap up the song in duet. Their fast tap numbers invariably pleased the crowds.

But they switched easily into the outrageously tacky roles of "Two Old Bags," with big holes in their hose and the high button shoes that never were buttoned right, and old Minnie Pearl hats.

★ Francis Blair perfected his impersonation in Seattle cabarets and burlesque houses during the Depression.

When Blair was at the Garden, he'd always close the show in the star spot. The finale was a "Tra-la-la-boom-de-a" type of number, Drake said. When he danced, it might be a Betty Grable hula routine to "Little Grass Shack." He might sing "Hula Lu," "Hard-hearted Hannah," an old Garden blue song of Eppe Waters, "My Handy-

★ Blair was a polished and lovely Prima Donna.

man," or "Henry Ford": "Will you love me when my body is a wreck, when my pistons stop piston, my spark plugs stop sparking…"

Blair's reputation spread nationwide when Walter Winchell, the syndicated columnist, mentioned "the boy with the million-dollar legs." Countess Estelle remembered his gorgeous costumes, including some made for Hedy Lamarr that he bought in Hollywood.

During the Korean War, Blair performed in drag in several USO shows. Once, Countess Estelle said, he was stripping and was wearing only a G-string when the USO hostess "had a fit and put a stop to it." The same hostess, a very proper English woman, also accused Countess Estelle of being in the show under false pretenses. "I am not! I always take off my wig at the end of the show," he retorted.

Blair had maintained his membership in the dishwashers' union so he would have employment between shows. Once, while he was washing dishes in a restaurant in the Broadway Market in Seattle, he accepted an offer to return to Finocchio's in San Francisco. On that stage, he had played both a glamorous Prima Donna and a camp comedian in a routine with Kenny Bee. That time, the only offer was to reprise one of "The Two Old Bags from Oakland." Blair did the shows with his usual flair for low com-

★ Francis Blair's versatility is shown in this composite of his many roles. Clockwise, from lower left, a Prima Donna, an old Bag from Tacoma (Blair removed his false teeth for a Seattle performance, but once refused to do so in San Francisco), in male attire in the McCarthy era when female impersonation was temporarily banned, a Gay Nineties Prima Donna, leading a female chorus line, and a bathing-beauty Dame. (Composite by Don Paulson)

★ Hotcha Hinton signed this picture, "Last of the Red Hot Mamas." It was a characteristic look that she called the Flo Ziegfeld pose. Hinton performed for more than fifty years, and was relentless in insisting that she be taken as and treated as a woman.

edy, but when the director asked him to remove his false teeth as part of the act, pride stopped him; he refused.

Years later, while on a vacation trip, Blair and his lover of twenty years were attacked in Golden Gate Park in San Francisco. His lover and their dog were killed;

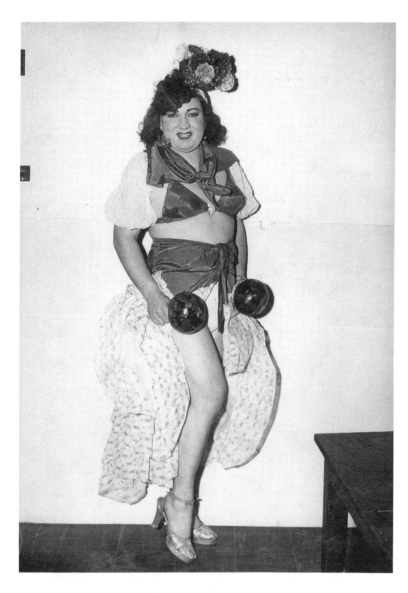

★ Hinton was loud and crude, but she knew how to put herself over to an audience. She made her own costumes, and those of other performers, as well.

Blair ran from the attackers and escaped injury. Devastated, he began a solitary drive back to the Northwest and was killed in a car crash in Oregon.

HOTCHA HINTON

Of all the performers at the Garden of Allah, Hotcha Hinton was the most outrageous and perhaps the most criticized. Still performing in her sixties, Hinton liked to say, "Honey, you gotta love life and it'll love you back. That's my philosophy and it keeps me young. I think young and I have young lovers. I can still kick over my head."

★ Hotcha Hinton stood on the left in this fearsome group of pirates. Also, from left, Jackie Starr, Robin Raye, and Billy DeVoe.

She was born June 12, 1915, began dancing in Chicago clubs when she was sixteen, and never stopped performing until her death at sixty-eight in 1983. She was one of the last survivors of the hardy breed of burlesque comedians. She once claimed that she had forty scrapbooks of clippings about her travels, but I've only been able to find one.

In 1980, she told a Davenport, Iowa, newspaper reporter: "I've traveled so much that I've never had the chance to marry and settle down, but I have no regrets. I'll be doing this until the day I die. The siren song of the road cannot be ignored. I can't live without the crowd, without the applause."

★ The Garden's version of "Miss America" featured, from left, Francis Blair, Kenny Bee, Hotcha Hinton, Jackie Starr, and Billy DeVoe.

Hinton was born in a theater trunk. Her mother, an aerialist with the Sells Floto Circus, was a wild number, a good mother, and at ninety-two still played golf and bet on jai-alai games in Florida.

At the age of seven, Hinton took dancing lessons from Buddy Ebsen's father. She met Ebsen when he jerked sodas on a Daytona Beach pier. Hayward Hinton—"Hotcha" came from a Broadway show—worked in the chorus line on the midway carnival, where Gypsy Rose Lee and Sally Rand were headliners, at the Chicago World's Fair in 1933. She also worked in the 1933 revue, *The Streets of Paris*, at the My

★ To capture the holiday spirit in 1974, Hinton put 168 lights on her dress, plugged herself into an electrical outlet, and poured on the cheer.

Oh My Club in Miami. When the big vaudeville theaters began to close, Hinton moved into burlesque, and performed in theaters and clubs all over the country. In 1938, she appeared in the burlesque musical *Vogues*. She knew Mae West, and most of the big-time strippers, including Rose LaRose, Gypsy Rose Lee, Madge Carmyle, Sally Rand, Lily St. Cyr, and Flame Fury. Sally Rand was the best, she often said. In 1971, she played a madam in a Hollywood film, *Lady Godiva Rides*. In later years, she often performed for college audiences. "Young people appreciate the time-tested and sometimes risque burlesque routines as much as their parents and grandparents did," she said.

She thought herself lucky for having good-looking legs. In her sixties, she bragged

★ Hotcha Hinton "Waiting for the Last Roundup" in 1982. This is the last picture taken of her during a performance; she fell ill soon after.

she still could pass Flo Ziegfeld's famous test for girls for his shows. He'd place three silver dollars in three places between their legs—between the thighs, the knees, and the calves. If the dollars stayed in place, the girls would be considered.

She lamented often that women entering the business didn't know their left foot from their right because they weren't trained dancers as she was. She scoffed at style-less routines, lack of talent, and the urge to take everything off. "The strippers I know," she told the Iowa reporter, "don't take it all off and that makes them more sexy. Some-thing is left for the imagination. I think a lot of people are tired of all that nudity and enjoy a novelty act like mine more."

She charmed and fooled both her audiences and her interviewers into seeing her as a woman. Her desire to be accepted as a woman was so strong that she simply failed to tell people she was a man. However, a close friend said she never wanted to change physically into a woman.

Friends say she was always generous and ready to help. She claimed that she got as many as five hundred Christmas cards. She was convinced that there was some good in everyone, and told her audiences to help each other out. She did benefits for many causes, especially for disabled persons. Her support for the Democratic Party led to fund-raisers for John Kennedy and Jimmy Carter. She corresponded with Lillian Carter, the former President's mother, and sent her twenty-four scrapbooks of clippings of her son's work. She said the biggest thrill of her life was going to a Carter inaugural ball with the stripper Flame Fury, who was best known for the "educated tassles" which she could flip in opposite directions. If Carter had been re-elected, she mused, maybe she and Flame would have slept in Lincoln's bed.

Her parting words to the Iowa newspaper reporter:

"I say my prayers every night to ask that I'll continue to be able to work and to enjoy life. Burlesque will never die as long as there are people like myself around to keep it alive. I've had a wonderful and colorful life and if I die tomorrow the world doesn't owe me a thing. I'd do it all over again exactly the same way. The siren song of the road cannot be ignored. The show must go on."

I've chosen to remember Hotcha Hinton by sharing stories from those who worked with her. Time after time, as I interviewed her friends, I was taken by the powerful images they used to describe her.

JIMMY CALLEY

Hotcha was a burlesque slut. A chippy whore with no talent. She'd swish across the stage doing a loud, boisterous, dirty monologue pretending to be a cute little thing; a cutesy Mary Pickford in a whorehouse. But, she was a big fat cow. She couldn't sing, and she couldn't dance, looked like a cunt, had no talent; she was a floozy bag. Thick greasepaint, long eyelashes, fingernail polish as bright as possible. Once I saw her on the street. She was dressed in red, blue, yellow. My God, she looked like she fell off the circus train. Onstage she had nothing to sell. She was loud and crude, but she could put herself over, *that* she had talent for. She wanted people to like her, she demanded people like her. When she came out on the stage, everyone said, "Oh my God! What a hussy! What is this?" But by the end of her performance the audience loved her. They couldn't help it. Fat, brassy, dirty jokes flying by; somewhere Hotcha touched that place that made you like her. Hotcha was a showman. She sold snake oil and swampland and put magic mirrors in front of your eyes. Hotcha made people laugh, broke down their reservations. My God! She could sell anything, especially herself, which she did whenever the opportunity arose.

Hotcha told a joke about a man with a large stomach standing on a bus in front of a woman who was sitting down. The woman said, "If that stomach was on a woman, I'd know what it was." The man replied, "Madame, it was on a woman last night. How was it?" Tame by Hotcha's standards.

WANDA BROWN

Hotcha was flamboyant. I liked Hotcha, but she could be a little overbearing. But she was Hotcha, whatever you wanted to say, she was Hotcha! She was a lot of swish, but she didn't care. She did a little bit of everything on stage. But I think her weight had a lot to do with her performing style. She was quite heavy and I think the swishy things she did were to make up for her lack of physical beauty. She used mannerisms with her hands to keep people from looking too closely at her body. Hotcha was a very strong personality. She lived in drag, used electrolysis, and was only seen as a woman. She reminded me of a story-book madam, you know, the madam of the house in any western.

OLNEE, HOTCHA'S SISTER

Hotcha was always a go-getter and always involved in show biz. He went to St. Paul Catholic School in Daytona Beach, Florida, and was involved in all the school plays, played in them, made sets, and made all the costumes. He could have been a top designer. Of course, with his gift of gab he was a great emcee. Hayward was very outgoing, he knew how to have fun, much like the rest of our family, always cracking a joke or doing something to get people going. We're all like that. Hotcha never had an enemy, he was so good natured. When he was young, he'd sell newspapers, do errands for old people, work around wherever he could to get enough money to go to shows. Show business was in his veins. He loved it.

ROBY JACOME

One night at the Garden while I was maitre d', Hotcha was getting ready to go on and do her snake number, but no snake! Oh my God! A real live snake loose in the Garden of Allah! We looked and looked but no reptile anywhere. We all knew that if we didn't find the damn thing it was sure to come slithering across the floor during Jackie's quietest song and panic everybody. The show had to go on so Hotcha substituted some other outrageous number. After the performance as the cast were trying to calm down, Hotcha was about to sit down on a recliner hide-a-bed in the back office when I screamed, "Don't sit down!" If she had, Hotcha would have had a squashed dead snake instead of a healthy one. The creature had crawled into the folding works of the hide-a-bed, trying to find a little place to curl up and get warm. Hotcha and her blue indigo were reunited.

KIM DRAKE

I didn't like Hotcha. I never saw anything good in her. To me she acted like a big, overstuffed truck driver with too big feet who didn't know where she was going. She talked like a drunken sailor or a burly lumberjack. Hotcha was a "dirty worker," in showbiz talk. If she didn't have those snakes, she'd been a nothing.

One night I got on Hotcha's list. I introduced her act and I said, "To keep the show going we had to get someone who just spent the last five weeks working with a donkey." Hotcha almost killed me she was so mad. She took lipstick and wrote on my mirror, "Die, Bitch!" Oh, God, she hated me after that. I don't blame her. Jackie was my protector; she'd say, "He's only doing it for a laugh," but Hotcha was not amused.

I thought of her as a minority because she was different than anyone else: fat, bawdy, outrageous costumes. I'd be horrified when she came down to the Garden with her three or four snakes, usually one large one. She would bring them into the dressing room and everyone would squirm and she'd count them and scream, "One's missing!" All evening you'd be afraid you'd sit on it or it would come crawling out from somewhere toward you. Hotcha would come out on stage dressed in chiffon and bells straight out of some crazy Arabian Nights with exotic music on the organ and practically having sex with that damned snake wrapped around her with its tongue darting out, and Hotcha's tongue touching the snake's. Jackie, Ricky, Robin Raye, and I were ladies. Hotcha was not a lady. We all prayed for April to come because Hotcha would go off to work the carnival and take her damn snakes with her!

SKIPPY LARUE

I met Hotcha for the first time at the Garden of Allah in 1947. The first words out of her mouth were: "Follow that guy into the men's room and see how big his dick is."

Hotcha came from a circus family in Daytona Beach, Florida. His parents separated when he was young and to make ends meet, Hotcha went to work in a Greek restaurant. He had sort of an exchange agreement with the cook. In return for letting the man smear Hotcha's ass with lard and fuck him, he could take home extra food for his brothers and sisters. He would wake up his brother and sister and make them eat; they didn't have much during the day. Those late night feasts always included chocolate milk.

There were three big days in Hotcha's life. Her birthday, June 12, Halloween, and Mardi Gras. She'd go south, throw her money away, come back flat broke, and always say, "Well, I had a good time; what were you doing for yourselves the last couple of weeks?"

You couldn't forget her birthday because she wouldn't let you. She'd always have a big party, fry some chicken or something. She was always feeding her friends fried chicken. Perhaps a trick she learned from that Greek cook? No matter where she was, she'd whip up a party, feed everyone just like she'd done for her brother and sister.

At your ringside table, all of a sudden Hotcha would come swishing across the dance floor full steam ahead for your attention, or else. Talking two miles a minute. "I've-been-sewing-all-day-slaving-away-on-some-new-costumes-all-covered-with-sequins-you'll-die-over-them-they're-so-gorgeous-when-I'm-through-and-that-new-pair-of-electric-scissors-are-so-fast-I'm-so-glad-I-bought-them-the-new-show-is-so-fabulous-with-these-new-costumes-I'm-doing-all-this-for you-because-I-know-how-you-love-the shows-here-and-*will-one-of-you-darlings-buy-me-a-drink-before-I-drop?*"

Throwing her arms over her head for the punch line. That routine always worked. The drinks and the applause came quickly. She had earned them once again. The applause from her friends, whether she knew them or not, was the acknowledgment Hotcha needed. And she got it. The Queen of Gay Burlesque had landed. Landed like a B-29. Stomping and swishing around that stage, she'd let those rough words and attitudes fly and if you didn't like them, she never noticed. Right on, like a steam train on the Fourth of July, Red, White and Blue, very BLUE. But unlike some professional comics, Hotcha wasn't mean. She was too good-natured to be mean. She was a lively wire. She was burlesque, that was her thing, her style, her energy. She lived for that rowdy laugh, that applause. And she always got it.

She had her dates, a lot of them, but show biz was her real love, first, foremost, and forever. She was always flamboyant. When she was in town at the Garden, we brought out the champagne. She could sell that stuff like food to a dying man.

You had to know Hotcha to love her. For those who never got that close, she was a little dangerous. And very dangerous if crossed by a rude, drunk heckler.

She didn't like to be reminded that she was really a male. If a telephone operator answered with "Yes, Sir," Hotcha would fly into a royal rage and scream into the phone, "I'm a woman; can't you tell a lady when you hear one?" Once in Great Falls, Montana, one of her competitors, Ray Bourbon, introduced her as Mr. Hotcha Hinton. Wrong. Hotcha was furious. "I'll kill that cocksucker." Both Ray Bourbon and Lee Leonard knew Hotcha's sensitive areas and since they were similar barrelhouse types, they enjoyed sticking it to her. She always returned it in kind.

But one on one, everybody treated her like a woman. Lady, no, but woman, yes. She was like Jackie and me in drag. She played the part. That was important. Everything Hotcha did she did in a hurry. But she put her energy to good use all around. She made all the finale costumes for the Garden shows. She'd zip up those costumes in no time, but for a show the sewing didn't have to pass close-up inspection. The costumes were just for flash and were not expected to last long. Hotcha loved glitter, sequins, rhinestones, anything that sparkled. I often wondered if she learned that from her childhood circus days. Once in 1974, she made a red satin dress she decorated with 168 Christmas tree lights. All those lights and a twenty-foot extension cord. She was the spirit of Christmas herself. As a birthday surprise for her three-year-old niece, Hotcha made a costume. It was the basic stripper's outfit, two pasties and a G-string. On a three-year-old.

There was an old guy who came down to the Garden wearing a pair of old overalls, work boots, faded shirt, etc. People wouldn't talk to him. So Hotcha goes up to the man and yells out, "Well, hello! This is my husband," and started carrying on with him. Well, he liked the attention and hung around for I don't know how many weeks. They worked him pretty good—Hotcha and Myrtle and Helen, who were patrons of the Garden. He'd buy drinks, donate toward costumes, and send up for hot dogs with the works from the hot dog stand at the top of the stairs. Turns out Hotcha's "husband" was just another miner from Alaska, who knew where to go to have a good time. One day, he just disappeared, probably back up north, flat broke, or at least as close to broke as Hotcha and friends could get him.

When Hotcha was living in Seattle in the late 1940s, she improved her business prospects by having three or four pimps to promote her. We used to kid her about having seventeen "husbands." She loved it. To her, her pimp, Big Bob, was a real man. Hotcha didn't like abuse but she liked being kept in line. Her pimp would give her a cuff or two and she would say to me later, "Ooooh, look at what he did to me." But it was never a physical abuse relationship. Hotcha liked to carry on about anything, anytime. Once she said she was going to commit suicide by jumping out the second-story window of the Willard Hotel. Big Bob suggested she go up a couple of floors so she wouldn't miss the sidewalk. Hotcha changed the subject. In time-honored tradition, Hotcha would lavish money on her promoters. Once she bought Big Bob a $500 suit. Another time she said she bought him an Arabian racehorse.

When Hotcha went into the hospital in those closing days, she changed into men's clothes. She spared herself and the hospital staff going through a big trip which would have been spread all over the hospital. So she checked in as a man. Hotcha would never let anyone see her out of drag, but an old friend came to see her at the hospital. I asked her, "Do you want him to see you out of drag?" She said, "That's okay." When Hotcha died, I had her cremated so when she went out she was in one of those androgynous hospital gowns. She was neither a man nor a woman. In death the sexes meet.

JACKIE STARR

I heard the name Jackie Starr several times before I saw the pictures in the steambath. It was already fixed in my mind that Jackie was a top star. Everybody else thought so too, and yet, to me, he was the most elusive and even the most mysterious personality at the Garden of Allah.

"There was something about Jackie," George Muzzy said, "like he knew a truth in life that no one else did. He was different from others at the Garden. Barbs about female impersonators just rolled off his back. He liked himself and nothing was going to interfere with his career."

When Starr came on stage the place became uncharacteristically silent, a sign of admiration and anticipation. Fred Reeves said that Starr was hypnotic on stage. "He had that mystique and gave the illusion of a perfect woman. He never went out of character. He simply did not look like a man in drag. He commanded respect."

Others noted his versatility. "Now I can see this beautiful brown-eyed woman standing there like a movie star and singing her theme song, 'As Time Goes By,'" Isaac Monroe said. "At another time, Jackie would come on stage as a ballerina, using his formal ballet training to become an aggressive, but supreme Prima Donna."

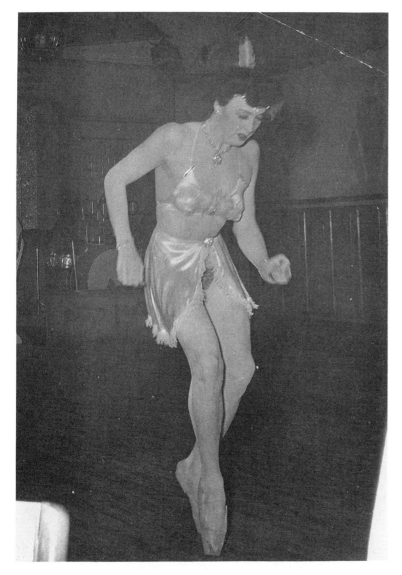

★ Jack Starr, trained for ballet, was one of the few entertainers who danced on point.

Richard Arbicore said that he and Virgil, his partner, loved Jackie very much. "He was a wonderful man, a man who liked to use people and you knew it, but because you loved him you really didn't mind." Arbicore said that Starr insisted on elegance in the things that surrounded him. "Always picture perfect. When Jack entered the room, whether he was in drag or not, there was always something that made him stand out."

Jack Starr was born May 9, 1915. Mona Thomas, a patron of the Garden and a friend, said that he had a normal Midwest farmboy childhood. "His parents apparently gave him encouragement to be an actor and he was well educated; in fact, Jackie was spoiled," she said. He studied acting and voice and had classical ballet training with a

★ With the look and manner of Gypsy Rose Lee, Jackie Starr completes a strip. He replaced Lee in at least two shows in New York City.

Russian teacher. "His sister Anna had a lot to do with raising him; she began dressing him in girls' clothes at age five."

Starr started doing drag in some of the mob-controlled speakeasies in Chicago in

1929. He performed solo, and sang as well as danced in the line of showgirls. He played the drag circuit in the 1930s, and made a grand tour of South America. Perhaps there, or on a European tour where he performed for royalty, he met a prince who wanted to give him everything if only he would go back to his country with him. Starr later told Mona Thomas, "I was tempted but I'm glad I didn't because he was killed in a coup and I'd have been killed too."

She said that Jackie went out with senators and other important people in Washington, D.C. "They'd always be sure Jackie had a razor to shave in the morning so he could leave in perfect drag."

In the 1930s, Jackie moved to Greenwich Village and tried acting and singing in straight night clubs. He had a strong tenor voice. He did some ballet in New York City, both straight and as a female impersonator. He was one of the few men in the world who danced on point at that time.

Several people said that the famous female stripper, Gypsy Rose Lee, fell ill one time and Jackie Starr took her place unannounced at an uptown music hall. The ruse was successful, and when the story broke in the newspapers, it did his career no harm. Lee asked him at least one other time to take her place in a show, a feat Starr accomplished with some deft changes in his makeup and hair. Photographs of Gypsy and Jackie, taken at the time, suggest the two could easily have changed places.

In the late 1930s Starr joined the *Jewel Box Revue*. Wanda Brown, a Seattle blues singer and Garden emcee, saw him perform in Minneapolis in 1938. "I saw Jackie in a Jeanette MacDonald and Nelson Eddy routine. They were singing 'Springtime' and Jackie, in drag, was Jeanette sitting in the swing." Starr was dating an Italian woman who roomed with Brown.

Starr was bisexual and had relationships with both men and women. In the 1930s, he danced as a Radio City Music Hall Rockette stand-in and was married briefly to one of the Rockettes. (When he came to the Garden he could still do that high kick, straight up.) In the 1940s, he moved to the West Coast, married again, and fathered a child.

He was in the merchant marine during the war, and then his agent signed him up for the Garden where he became its reigning star. Francis Blair must have been jealous. He was as much a pro as Starr was and also had fifteen years of experience as a female impersonator. Blair was respected for his talent, but he must have realized that he couldn't compete with Starr for looks. Starr was the perfect Prima Donna, a touch of mystery, a disarming style that captured the audience. His Prima Donna turns came late in the shows, often just before the finale in which he joined several other impersonators.

He gave class and dignity to a cabaret whose dynamic young performers were only learning the ropes of a dying craft. Maybe he went to Seattle because his age no longer gave him top spots. Melcohm McCay commented, "I think Jackie was past his peak when he came to Seattle. He was still active in his career but he had already done much of the important artistic work."

I wondered why he concentrated on female impersonation when he had so many

talents. I think the answer was in his looks. He was an average-looking leading man, but a spectacular woman. He and Skippy LaRue both found that the job market was far more lucrative when they played women. "I don't think Jack really wanted to go legitimate," Mona Thomas said. "He liked what he did and he was so damn good at it. He knew all along how good he was, he was the best and could have gone on to a wider career."

Jackie Starr was a headliner at the Garden for ten years. The young performers,

★ Jackie Starr relaxed in his apartment in the Governor Hotel in Seattle. One of his publicity shots was mounted on the wall.

many in their early twenties or younger, were in awe of the far greater experience of the veteran, who was thirty-six when the Garden opened, and took their cues from his perfected style. Harvey Goodwin, a female impersonator, said Starr sat in a bathtub with ammonia in the water to make his skin like velvet. He took painstaking care in every element of his performance—skin, makeup, wig, costume, voice, movement, dance, and at that time the ultimate signature of a Prime Donna, the strip. Swooping and prancing and teasing, he'd take off a bit of costume, wait for the effect, then doff something else. A deft comedian when the routines called for it, Starr thrived on the humor of the tease, playing the tension in the audience, boosting it, deflating

★ Jackie Starr and Bill Scott posed on their wedding day.

it with a comic gesture, calling it back again. And then he would be down to a G-string, one that gave no hint of the male sex that had to be there. Leaving the mystery unsolved, Jackie made a departing flourish to his fans, who would be standing, applauding wildly, whistling, and cheering. The minutes passed as "Sophisticated Lady" was played again and again; Bill Parkin said the strip sometimes lasted twenty minutes.

"We all had immense respect for Jackie's talent and person," Kim Drake, another impersonator, said, "but when he was in drag you didn't say a bad word because that might offend him. His mere presence, you felt you were in the presence of a real queen." Wanda Brown said that Starr didn't go out as many performers did. "He did his job and went home. He had his profession and he worked at it." Skippy LaRue added that Starr never "slept around" but was no angel either. "He knew his way around, but he was more the marrying type."

In the late 1940s, Bill Scott became the most prominent male in Starr's life. Scott was a homophobic bisexual truck driver and preacher who was married to Sister Faye, a street preacher who sold heroin on the side and ran a mission to help the poor,

★ Jackie Starr and Bill Scott had a wedding ceremony that bent all the gender rules. Jackie, in exquisite drag, and Bill kneeled after the ceremony performed by a Garden patron. Skippy LaRue, the impersonator maid of honor, stood behind Starr; the lesbian Nick Arthur, serving as best man, stood behind Scott.

wretched souls on Skid Road. Most of the funds, however, were injected into her veins. Scott helped at the mission and went door to door soliciting funds which never saw the light of charity. One day she just packed up and left town without Scott, who was shattered. (Later Sister Faye, high on heroin, was killed in a car accident.) Being something of a hustler himself, Scott connected with a now prominent gay man, who just wanted to sleep with him, but not live with him. In emotional turmoil, Scott wandered into the Garden of Allah one night and encountered the stage persona of Jackie Starr; it was love at first sight.

"Bill didn't like queers," Skippy LaRue recalled. "In fact, he hated them, but when he met Jackie his attitude changed right around and he got to love all the kids at the Garden. He looked at Jackie as a woman and he never looked at himself as being gay.

★ The cast and friends toasted Jackie and Bill in a friend's home.

If a gay man made an indiscreet pass at him he ended up on the floor." Scott had some rough edges but he knew when he met Starr that he had gone from trash to class.

Starr and Scott had a formal wedding and reception in the home of a friend, who played the part of a minister. Skippy LaRue was the maid of honor and Nick Arthur, a lesbian, was best man. After the reception, the bridal party went to an after-hours place and partied until 9 A.M. The next morning, the couple got into a fight.

Starr could be temperamental even though he had a sweet personality. Mona Thomas recalled going to the Governor Hotel for dinner with Starr and Scott. "When I approached their door I could hear a lot of commotion. Someone said, 'You dirty rotten…' and I heard something crash against the wall. Jack came to the door and said, 'Come in and sit down 'till we're through fighting!' " She continued: "In drag Jackie was always the perfect lady and straight he was the perfect gentleman. He never lost his temper in public, but in private when he lost his temper, especially with Bill, he wasn't feminine anymore. One night he knocked Bill out. I think that upset him because after that he fought more like a woman would. They'd both throw things and scuffle but they both held back, especially Bill because he was so strong he could have laid Jackie flat with one punch."

Friends said that Scott, like many straight men, liked to have Starr, the "woman," take charge of their daily affairs and run their apartment. Starr was the top in the sexual relationship, a trait he shared with many drags. Skippy LaRue said that Scott wasn't ready for sex with his new partner. "Bill came to me before they were married and asked, 'What will I do if Jackie wants to screw me?' I said, 'For God's sake, Bill, just lie back, spread your legs, and enjoy it.'"

The two men were lovers for years, and remained friends until Scott's death. Scott met a woman who was supposed to inherit a fortune and married her. Although he grew to love the woman, he never stopped loving Starr, friends say. "I think his plan was to get the money and spend it on Jackie," Skippy LaRue said. Starr probably played along with the scheme. "Jackie could be manipulative in his own way, he knew how to do it, but he would never rip you off, nothing even close to that," he said. The money, however, was never realized and the woman died. Scott and Starr resumed their relationship and even ran a restaurant together until it failed. Several years later, both of Scott's legs were amputated. Starr took care of him until he died. "I think their relationship was a good one," LaRue said. "Bill drank a lot and was hard to understand, but they were in love. Bill worshiped Jackie."

For the last ten years of his life, Starr lived rent-free near the Seattle-Tacoma International Airport, in a mobile home in the yard of a house owned by Mona Thomas. Richard Arbicore, who had carried beer at the Garden, lived nearby and helped Jackie. "Both Virgil and I gave him $125 a month, but we each asked Jackie not to tell the other. That was okay because we wanted him to be near us."

And once in a while, even in his seventies, Jackie Starr went out on the town in drag. "I'd come in," Dusty Harrison, his last lover, said, "and there he'd be, sitting on the piano bench, putting polish on his nails, the last touch before going out." Two hours earlier, Jackie had begun the long process of applying his makeup. Meticulous treatment over the years kept his skin pale and spotless. When they'd go to the Golden Crown, a downtown Seattle drag bar, the new generation of drags would crowd around.

"Halloween 1985," Richard Arbicore recalled, "we all decided to go to the Bingo hall on the Muckleshoot Indian reservation about forty miles south of Seattle. People who came in costume were eligible for a prize. They walked all around the hall, modeling their costumes. Jackie was elegantly dressed in a long dress, fur, and long rhinestone earrings. When he won first prize, no one would believe he was a man, not even the emcee. Finally Jack had to show his driver's license. The emcee announced, 'Ladies and gentlemen, you're not going to believe this, but this very elegant beautiful woman next to me is a seventy-four-year-old grandfather.' Three hundred people went bananas. They must have applauded two minutes. It was unbelievable how they carried on. When Jack sat down to play Bingo no one would leave him alone. They wanted to touch his face, his legs, his hands—he had beautiful hands and nails. The women didn't want to play Bingo; they were all after Jack. That was Jackie's sense of humor, toying with the crowd at a Bingo parlor."

Dusty Harrison's dinner parties for Starr drew all the gang from the Garden and

★ Jackie Starr posed in four of his costumes and roles (pages 160–163). (Photos courtesy of Rita Kelsey)

were occasions for recreating the best times from that era. Dinners were also important for Starr and Jim Gerlach, a friend for more than forty years. "We'd get together for dinner, listen to music of the 1940s, or go to a showing of an old movie like *Casablanca*. Sometimes we'd go to a bar and dance, two old fools out there dancing, getting drunk, plotting. Sometimes we'd go walking and nudge each other as a good-

looking guy passed us, just like we did forty years before, a couple of kids having fun, being silly, getting the most out of life."

In 1981, Jackie Starr and Dusty Harrison became lovers, although Starr also had relationships with three women in that period. "Jack was very sensitive, discreet, and thoughtful," Harrison said. "He was always aware of other people's needs. He was the kind of man anyone would want to marry or be around."

Harrison described a man who loved velvet, fine jewelry, antiques, and classical music. "We'd go to plays at the Seattle Repertory Theatre and concerts—we never missed *The Messiah*. Jack wrote songs and played the piano, especially the semiclassics. He was a handsome man and a gentleman and I was always proud to be seen in public with Jack Starr. When he went out in drag at age seventy he was a lady, and I used to enjoy seeing unknowing people treat him like one. Jack was never apologetic about his background. He was a pro and he was proud of what he did.

He felt that others would just have to handle it if it bothered them. He was too upbeat for negativity."

Harrison added, "He was not political, but he despaired at today's violence. He was concerned about corruption and vice and especially the plight of the poor and the street people. He was sad for their lack of continuity. For Jack, life was rhythmic. He lived with compassion. He never complained; he was courageous right to the end. He was a wonderful man and I and many others will always love him dearly."

chapter *9*

EPILOGUE

★

The last days of the Garden of Allah were troubled. The cabaret in the Arlington's basement no longer drew gay men and lesbians in great numbers, no longer nurtured the seeds of community, no longer seemed to be the oasis of safety that it had been right after the war. The Garden had played a vital role in defining Seattle's gay and lesbian community, but then the pressures on the Garden destroyed its capacity to thrive, and gays and lesbians went elsewhere.

The musicians' union made more demands, the city levied heavier cabaret taxes, and the police continued to use the payoff system as an extra-legal tax on gay businesses. The state legalized liquor by the drink, depriving beer and wine clubs of much of their appeal. Officers showed up more often to intimidate managers and patrons. The Garden was closed for thirty days for selling beer to a minor, and in a rare gay-bar raid, the police booked four impersonators and the bartender on the suspicion of having dope and allowing minors in the Garden and then closed it briefly.

In the climate of suspicion associated with Senator Joseph McCarthy in the early 1950s, the military kept the Garden off limits to servicemen. Police would drop in with light meters because if it was too dark surely people would be doing nasty things under the tables. A local board began to censor some of the more racy songs and dialogue. For awhile Lee Leonard and Ray Bourbon were banned from the Garden by the censor board, and at times the Garden wasn't allowed to have drag at all. To keep the shows going, Francis Blair organized a girlie review, using his burlesque chorus-line friends. To appease the authorities, Blair, the Garden's talented Prima Donna, had to dress as a man.

Countess Estelle remembered, "During the McCarthy era, there were some screwy rules concerning drags, things like you had to wear men's underwear under your drag costume and carry ID on you at all times, even on stage. Also you could not be glamorous—you had to do or wear something that would destroy the illusion."

The liquor board had imposed a rule calculated to annoy both owners and customers. The law forbade a patron standing while

★ In the McCarthy era, drag shows were stopped by city authorities. Francis Blair, the Garden's star Prima Donna, organized a revue using women from the Rivoli Burlesque Theatre chorus line.

drinking, but the owners were afraid someone would forget and take a sip while moving about, so drinks couldn't even be carried from table to table.

By 1956, the Garden had been around for ten years and the novelty of female impersonators had worn thin. (Indeed, no drag was performed in Seattle for five years after the Garden closed.) New gay bars drew off jaded patrons, and it became harder to keep the shows going. Kim Drake, a female impersonator who sang and stripped at the Garden, recalled: "I think we entertainers weren't keeping the acts up and then they stopped bringing acts in. It got to be a matter of the same people putting on the same shows, same songs, same old jokes. After about 1954 everybody just seemed to scatter."

And a new kind of drag already was eclipsing the classic female impersonation offered by the Garden. Throughout the country, drags were moving their lips to recordings. They were just as glamorous as the impersonators, but they no longer needed the talent to sing and dance. Because of costly union demands, cabarets, losing customers to television, no longer could afford costly backup music. The Prima Donna became a lonely figure who had no voice. Overnight, amateurs took over the profession of female impersonation, barely keeping it alive in gay bars.

Reid and Carlburg, the owners, had grown tired. They began holding brunches on Saturdays to drum up business that might stay into the evening. Since food couldn't legally be given away, the Garden charged a nominal twenty-five cents a meal, but even that tactic didn't help.

No one remembered clearly about the closing of the Garden; I'd like to think there was a gigantic party with a special floor show and official closing ceremonies. At first, the space was used to store survival rations in case of nuclear attack. In the next few years, the former Garden was a biracial rock venue called the House of Entertainment, where Jimi Hendrix played. It also served as a jazz club and a meeting house for a black church. A film company made *Cinderella Liberty* in deserted rooms of the hotel in the early 1970s, but the Garden's space was rarely used. Preservationists tried to save the historic building but it fell to the wrecking ball in 1974.

So, the Arlington Hotel is gone, but not the knowledge of the profound role it played in fostering a lively, self-confident community of gay men and women of all ages. The noisy dishing at the tables, the bravado Prima Donna performances, the bizarre tableau of police officers standing guard in defiance of community mores to guarantee Jackie Starr's right to strip are lasting memories of that special place. The payoff system allowed gay men and lesbians to gather in a protected establishment that public opinion might otherwise not have tolerated.

The Garden closed before the police protection system, which had been so vital to its success, reached its own end. By the 1960s the entrenched system was taking some heat. Angry citizens and city visitors wrote City Hall from time to time asking for action, but the letters were either filed and forgotten or sent off for replies to the very officers in the Police Department who were running the system. In 1966, the Federal Bureau of Investigation notified the City of Seattle that it had been monitoring the police payoff system for years. Among its informants were owners of Seattle gay taverns. It was two gay bar owners who first complained to the FBI in 1959 that liquor inspectors and beat cops were forcing them to make weekly payoffs for protection, and they provided more information over the years. In 1967 the *Seattle Times* published the first major investigation of the payoff system and its effect on gay bars, and the palace began to crumble. In time, the payoff system was broken with convictions and forced resignations of officers. The courage of the gay bar owners was briefly noted in the newspapers, then too quickly forgotten.

The defining quality of the Garden, too, was the bravery of its performers and audience. Butches and impersonators have always been the figureheads of the gay movement.

The impersonators turned the Prima Donna and the Dame into repositories of gay language, experience, and attitude. Against the encroaching tide of television, voiceless lip-synching drags, and rock, they kept small flames of resistance glowing. They respected the pain of people who had been vilified and ignored; they created a rite of passage for men and women who came to the Garden as a step outside the closet of social stigma. They voiced a consciousness of defiance against the hate and disdain of the street and workplace. Lesbians and gays found inspiration in those moments.

Decades later, they spoke with great affection of the turn-of-the-century tile floor and the palm trees and stars stenciled on the walls. But as they warmed to the story, one heard much more—the noise of the crowd, the roar of the organ, the emcee's raunchy intro, the silence when Jackie entered.

It was their crowd, their music, their Jackie and Hotcha and Francis. It was a nightly gathering that spawned a thousand parties, jokes, and brassy retorts. Once one had the courage to step through its door, to move from the relative silence of First Avenue into the incredible sounds of the Garden—a merging of the organ's bellow and the voices of gay men and lesbians expressing themselves without inhibition—the Garden repaid the risk in diamonds. The Garden was not a meetinghouse for gay liberationists, but it was the crucible in which lesbians and gay men formed and refined their ideas about repression, identity, and resistance. The crucible allowed them to find the meaning in the painfully contradictory experiences of being kicked around on the street and making a workable society inside the Garden.

One result was a Seattle gay and lesbian community that has steadily gained recognition and acceptance over two decades. Helped by an early-1970s alliance with city government, the Seattle community has fought off two drives aimed at weakening gay and lesbian rights, led in the health establishment's fight against AIDS in the region, and formed a wealth of fine musical, business, artistic, political, athletic, religious, charitable, and other organizations.[*]

As I picked up the trail of the Garden of Allah a few years back, I realized that information about it was fading quickly. In no time, the cabaret would have become just an obscure name in Seattle history. Well, now its story is known. It satisfies me that although I had never been in the Garden, I was able to answer the question: "What was the Garden of Allah?"

Stephen Blair, a Seattle Democratic Party gay-issues activist, told me that the Garden offered him healing from the wounds of war and family conflict. "It released some of the hurt because you could laugh. It was one of the few places gays could laugh at themselves."

Rita Kelsey wrote me that the Garden was paradise. "In it we found love, understanding, companionship, friendship, and a common bond. We were more or less one big family." I've come to understand how that cabaret could be transformed through memories into, in Kelsey's phrase, "our palace of dreams." Gay existence often calls on the fantasy that someday there will be a world of comfort, support, and love. That was the dream. The Garden was the place where one could find the will to stand up to the reality of prejudice. The Garden of Allah was the oasis before the challenging journey across the hot desert. I agree so much with Kelsey who wrote, "I feel blessed to have lived in the time and age of it and to have experienced the happiness and love that I found there."

---

[*]Police harassment of men in drag ceased when Jim Faggley, a gay bar owner, complained to the new mayor, Wes Uhlman, that there was no law on the books forbidding cross-dressing in public. "No more harassment," Uhlman told the police chief.